DEAD MEN WALKING
HOW TO DIE TO SELF

By VICKIE FAURIE

CREATION
HOUSE PRESS
A STRANG COMPANY

DEAD MEN WALKING by Vickie Faurie
Published by Creation House Press
A Strang Company
600 Rinehart Road
Lake Mary, Florida 32746
www.creationhouse.com

Unless otherwise noted, scripture quotations are from the Holy Bible, New International Version. Copyright © 1973, 1978, 1984, International Bible Society. Used by permission.

Cover design by Mark Labbe

Library of Congress Control Number: 2004109824
International Standard Book Number: 1-59185-646-9

04 05 06 07 08 — 987654321
Printed in the United States of America

This book and poem are lovingly dedicated to the Holy Trinity, with special thanks to the Holy Spirit who inspired and enabled the writing of this book.

How great is God, yet how small am I.
I am just a mere vessel, upon the altar of sacrifice.
O God of endless love, let the rivers of life flow through me.
As I embrace the cross and run the race that's set before me.

—VICKIE FAURIE

ACKNOWLEDGMENTS

WITH A HEARTFELT gratitude to those who imparted God's Word into my life, I want to acknowledge them for their contribution. With love and gratitude to my dear husband, Gary, whom I deeply appreciate for his sacrifice in getting this book out. To my wonderful children, who are all unique and treasured gifts from God. And to my parents for raising me in a home that taught me about God. I want to especially acknowledge Pastors Billy Joe and Sharon Daugherty of Victory Christian Center in Tulsa, Oklahoma. Thank you for allowing me to share this message a few times at Victory as I wrote this book. With gratitude to LeSea Broadcasting in Southbend, Indiana, for interviewing me and allowing me to share about *Dead Men Walking*. A special thank you to Sid Roth, and his part in allowing me to share on radio and television the message contained in this book and my testimony. I want to acknowledge the part that Kathryn Kuhlman had in my life and thank God for being raised up off a deathbed of affliction to share His message to the body of Christ. To all of those at Creation House, thank you for your contribution in this project and your prayerful support.

CONTENTS

Introduction   1

1 Absolutely Surrendered   3

2 The Altar, the Water, and the Cross   11

3 Godlessness or Godliness?   15

4 Dead to Sin—Alive to God   23

5 Keys to God's House   33

6 Ignited Passion Through Intimacy   41

7 Perseverance Has a Price   49

8 Belief vs. Obedience   57

9 Fear of the Lord—a Holy Reverence   67

10 Committed or Compromising?   75

11 Where Is Your Heart?   83

12 Imitators of God (Followers)   91

13 Abiding in God's Presence and Manifested Glory   99

14 Ears to Hear   109

15 Examine Yourself As You Run the Race   117

16 The Father's Will or Yours?   123

17 Unlocking the Power: Prayer and Fasting   129

18 God Inhabits Your Praises   141

Notes   147

INTRODUCTION

ARE WE SO blinded by Satan the deceiver that we are failing to see what God truly wants? Is He in search of dead men walking? Dead men are free from sin. No sin abounds, for they have crucified the flesh and entered into a reconciled relationship (absolutely joined together) with Christ. They are dead to sin, yet alive unto God.

The Spirit of God is breathing upon His people and giving revelation knowledge to us in a detailed plan so illuminating that, if we live according to His perfect plan and completely believe, it will transform us totally.

Though it may seem overwhelming at first, when we begin to examine ourselves deeper, we might even begin to think it can never happen. Wrong, wrong, wrong! We need to get our minds off of self. Self must die—die and be dead to the things of this world. Get to the point where God is 100 percent

1

in control, and your mind will be set on Him alone. Total obedience to the Master is required.

We need to enter into that holy place where self is no longer exalted, but where Christ *is* exalted. Are we ready? Are we truly ready to become as walking dead men? There is a price to pay, and very few have ever given up all for Christ Jesus. God is waiting to see who will apply for the position of "dead men walking."

Romans 6:11–12 says, "In the same way, count yourselves dead [*live the crucified life*] to sin, but alive to God in Christ Jesus [*abiding and dwelling in Christ Jesus*]. Therefore do not let sin reign in your mortal body so that you obey its evil desires. [*This is a command when it says do not let sin reign.*]" (emphasis added).

In Matthew 16:24, "Then Jesus said to his disciples, 'If anyone would come after me [*seek me and pursue me*], he must deny himself [*die to self*] and take up his cross [*crucify the fleshly nature of man*] and follow me [*be imitators of Christ's divine nature*]'" (emphasis added).

Chapter 1

ABSOLUTELY SURRENDERED

WHEN WE REALIZE the deep joy and pleasure found in the crucified life, turning from sin completely, denying self, giving up in absolute surrender to Christ, and walking in total obedience and the will of God become deep joy as we abide in Him. Absolute surrender is how Jesus Christ lived and remains today. As our living example, He totally yielded Himself to the Father, and He calls us to die to self and surrender ourselves, giving all of ourselves to the Father. This turning from sin—separating ourselves from the things of this world—is expressing our commitment to live only for God our creator. Death to self is the narrow road, and the enemy continually tries to set up traps to entangle the believer trying to crucify their self.

Let's take a look at the lives of two men of God who had to learn the crucified life. It will shed a great deal of more light on how it is possible to live this life. First, let's examine the life of the apostle Paul. Paul, who was then known as Saul, was present at the stoning of Stephen (Acts 7:58). Saul was known for killing the believers of Christ. In Acts 9, Saul had an encounter with Jesus on the road to Damascus. An amazing conversion process began in the life of Saul, now named Paul the Apostle. Reading 2 Corinthians 12:7–9 will shed some more light on the life of Paul: "To keep me from being conceited [*self-reigning in me*] because of these surpassingly great revelations, there was given me a thorn in my flesh, a messenger of Satan, to torment me. Three times I pleaded with the Lord to take it away from me. [*Paul knew that the Lord could remove this from Him.*] But he said to me, 'My grace [*divine assistance*] is sufficient for you, for my power is made perfect in weakness.'" God was saying, "No, Paul, I cannot remove this thorn from you, for then you would not depend upon Me. You would become conceited with yourself and exalt yourself. This was sent to you to keep you humble, emptied of self, and totally dependent upon my power and strength, not your own abilities."

Paul learned to rejoice in his weakness, for then he depended on Christ for his true strength. The apostle Paul goes on to say in verse 11, "Even though I am nothing." He had learned he was nothing and had to die to self. "Your attitude should be the same as that of Christ Jesus: Who, being in very nature God, did not consider equality with God something to be grasped, but made himself nothing" (Phil. 2:5–7). Then, in Philippians 3:7–8, Paul makes the statement, "But whatever was to my profit I now consider loss for the sake of Christ. What is more, I consider everything a loss compared to the surpassing greatness of knowing Christ Jesus my Lord, for whose sake I have lost all things."

The apostle stated that what he once counted as profit, he no longer considered profitable. Except knowing, abiding, dwelling with Christ the Lord, everything else was rubbish and he gladly considered it all a welcomed loss. Paul counted only Christ as valuable. The things of this world held no more value, for he had died to self and the desires thereof.

In Matthew 4:18–20, Jesus is walking along the Sea of Galilee. He sees two fishermen, Peter and Andrew, casting their nets into the water. He calls to the two brothers, "Come, follow Me, and I will make you fishers of men." Immediately, they left and followed Jesus. In Matthew 19:27, Peter says to Jesus, "We have left everything to follow you!" Peter was making it known that he had forsaken all to follow Jesus. This disciple went on to ask Jesus, "What then will there be for us?" He was wondering if he would receive anything beneficial from following Christ Jesus. He would learn, in time, the benefits far outweighed what he had given up to follow Christ. Peter was devoted and ready to obey the commands of Jesus. Matthew 14:28–29 tells us how Peter took courage: "'Lord, if it is you,' Peter replied, 'tell me to come to you on the water.' 'Come,' he said. Then Peter got down out of the boat, walked on the water and came toward Jesus." At the voice of Jesus telling Peter to come, he obeyed immediately. We know, as this story continues, Peter began to sink because his focus turned to the conditions around him. Later in the life of Peter, as we read in Matthew 16:15–17, Jesus asks, "Who do you say I am?" Peter answers, "You are the Christ, the Son of the living God." Jesus replies, "Blessed are you, Simon son of Jonah, for this was not revealed to you by man, but by my Father in heaven." Peter received the spiritual insight into who Christ was from the Father in heaven. In Matthew 16:21–24, Jesus predicts His death to the disciples. Peter, taking Jesus aside, says, "This shall never be. This shall never happen to you!" Jesus turns to Peter and replies, "Get behind me, Satan! You are a stumbling block to me; you do not have in mind the things of God, but the things of men." Then Jesus said to the disciples, "If anyone would come after me, he *must deny himself* and take up his cross and follow me" (emphasis added). Peter was trusting in his self-will when he said this shall not happen. Christ, recognizing Peter's self-will, rebuked him by saying, "You do not understand the things that be of God right now, but those of men. So therefore get behind me, Satan." Christ immediately follows up with the instructions for denying self and taking up the cross of Christ to follow Him. Peter had not understood the "death to self" life, or abiding in the cross with Christ. He knew he was following after Jesus as he walked upon earth and that he was in training, but he could not understand what was going to happen.

Jesus foretells Peter's disowning Him at the Last Supper ,recorded in Matthew 26:33–34. Peter says, "Even if all fall away on account of you, I never will." Jesus answered, "I tell you the truth, this very night, before the rooster crows, you will disown me three times." In Luke 22:31–34, Jesus says, "Simon, Satan has asked to sift you as wheat [*you are going to be tested*]. But I have prayed for you, Simon, that your faith may not fail. And when you have turned back from your sin, strengthen your brothers." Peter replies, "Lord, I am ready to go with you to prison and to the death." Jesus tells Peter, "I tell you, Peter, before the rooster crows today, you will deny three times that you know me."

In Matthew 26:69–75 and Luke 22:54–60, we read that Peter follows at a distance while Jesus is led into the house of the high priest. As Peter sits in the middle of the courtyard, a servant girl comes to him and says, "You were with Jesus of Galilee." Peter quickly denies knowing Him. A short while later, he is recognized again by someone who says, "This fellow is one of them with Jesus of Nazareth." A second time he denies Jesus, this time with an oath, stating, "I do not know the man!" The third time he is approached they say, "Surely you are one of them, for your accent gives you away." Peter swears to them, "I do not know the man!" Immediately the rooster crows. In that instant the Lord turns and looks at Peter, and Peter recalls the words Jesus had spoken to him: "Before the rooster crows today, you will disown me three times."

Immediately Peter went outside and wept bitterly, repenting

for his sin of disowning Jesus. Peter had stood by disowning Jesus who was about to be crucified. The reality of rejecting Jesus was now unveiled as the rooster crowed and the words of Jesus were all coming true before him. His overwhelming sorrow caused him to weep bitterly over his sin. Jesus was crucified, and Peter did nothing to save Him. After three years of following Jesus in blessed fellowship day in and day out, one of the selected disciples denied his Lord. Then we read in Luke 24:34–35, "'It is true! The Lord has risen and has appeared to Simon.' Then the two [on the Emmaus road] told what had happened on the way, and how Jesus was recognized by them when he broke the bread."

The joy of knowing that Jesus was alive was delight to Peter's being. In John 21:15–17, Jesus reinstates Peter as He asks him, "Do you truly love Me more than these [*People or things in this world*]?" Peter replies, "Yes, Lord, You know that I love You." Jesus instructs Peter to feed His people. Jesus asks, "Do you truly love Me [*am I first place*]?" Peter answers, "Yes, Lord, You know that I love You." Jesus tells Peter, "Take care of My people." The third time Jesus asks Peter, "Do you love Me?" Peter is hurt because Jesus asked for a third time, "Do you love Me?" Peter replies this time with, "Lord, You know all things; You know that I love You."

Peter knew nothing was hidden from Jesus. He knew He must die to self and choose to live in the crucified life. He was a follower of Christ and loving Him truly. By reading about Peter and Paul, we see through their lives the deliverance from self. The same deliverance is made available to us. As you thought of absolutely surrendering yourself, submitting your life fully to God, were you not brought to the end of self? The willpower of man surrendered to God's perfect will enables you to die to self, giving God control. Put yourself fully into His hands in total surrender of yourself.

My personal experience on how to live the crucified life came about through deep searching and praying to God for help. My Christian walk was difficult, for I continually was seeking the blessings of God while I was living my own self-will in disobedience to His commands. I stood on the promises of the Word, but received very little of those promises due to being unsurrendered to God completely. Total obedience and surrender to God was not what my strong-willed being was ready to embrace, let alone understand the meaning or process of submission. I had said the prayer of salvation, knew some of the Word, and knew that God was real. I was raised in church and was taught salvation consisted of asking Jesus into your heart and being forgiven of your sins. I knew more than the basics of the Word, but still lacked understanding about the surrendered life to Christ. The life I previously pursued seemed to be founded upon religious formulas. I was now determined to have an intimate relationship of dwelling daily with Christ. In a simple childlike prayer, I asked God to reveal the condition of my heart and then to give me a heart like Jesus. I prayed the same prayer, asking God to reveal any sin in my heart and give me a heart like Jesus. This prayer was answered quickly as God started revealing the idols in my life. He gave me scriptures that listed my sinful condition, and then He told me the choice was mine whether to turn from sinning or not.

The cleansing and turning from sin, humbling before Him, was my free choice to make. My goal was to put God first above all else. I was determined that as Jesus was fully submitted to God, obeying and doing only the will of the Father must be the call of the Christian. Commandments such as, "Have no other gods before Me," "Seek first My kingdom," "Love the Lord your God with all your heart, all your soul, and all your mind," resounded through me. God was asking, "Am I truly first in your life? Do you really love Me?"

The Holy Spirit revealed the Word of God to my spirit man, showing and revealing the way God called His people to walk. My willpower and my fleshly nature needed to submit completely to the crucified life in which we are all called to live in. The death to self, daily crucifying the flesh and abiding in the cross with Christ, yet alive in Him, became reality through the Word of God. Totally surrendered to God, my will surrendered to His perfect will for me. The life that Christ revealed to man was to count ourselves as nothing, submitting fully to God, obeying Him only, and abiding in God with all the fruits of His Spirit. My deepest desire became following Him completely.

My prayer daily is to keep abiding in the cross of Christ, fully submitted to God my Father and obeying His commands. If I grieve or displease His heart, I ask that He grieve my heart. The position of a dead woman walking for Christ is the narrow road I have chosen. I pray you make application for the position and choose to die to self—daily abiding in the cross of Christ—fully submitted to the will of the Father.

> *Lord, my God, the prayer of my heart is to be dead to self, daily abiding in the cross, crucifying the flesh in total surrender to you. Lord, You have commanded me to take up my cross daily and follow You. To empty myself of my worldly ways, to not be of the world but set apart to reflect Christ in me to those around me. Lord, with joy I take up the cross of dying to my selfish will and humbly submit myself in total obedience to You, yielding to You and Your perfect will for me. Lord, I seek to be absolutely surrendered to You in every area of my life. Lord, thank You for hearing my prayer. Amen!*

Chapter 2

THE ALTAR, THE WATER, AND THE CROSS

DO YOU LONG for the blessed life, rich and fully yielded to God?

Once you learn to place your entire being on the altar of sacrifice, you will launch into a new way of living in Him. The altar of sacrifice, the water of life, and the blood of the cross all work together in a three-part cord which binds you to Christ Jesus.

The complete surrendering of oneself—mind, body, soul, and spirit—is all it takes. Simply put, dying to self is giving God your entire being on the altar of sacrifice.

Jesus, our blessed living example, came in the flesh to show us that the temptation of the flesh can be conquered through submission to God. (See Hebrews 2:14–18.) Jesus came in the form of man to teach us how to live in total submission to God. Every day, Jesus had to take up His cross and follow His Father's will. He lived His life moment by moment in a ceaseless yielding to the Father. Each day He lost His own life and will by dying to self, then speaking, doing, and following after everything He heard from His Father.

Jesus' ministry ranged from temptations, starting in the wilderness, to teaching and instructing the disciples, to His agony in the Garden of Gethsemane. He was tempted by the sin of self-assertion, but He overcame, for He understood He was subject only to the will of His Father. Our example, Jesus, who offered up His life, denied Himself, and took up His cross in total obedience to the Father, calls us to the same life.

The way to life in the fullness of God is through yielding yourself to Him. You have the choice to lose your life—or hold on to your life. Jesus chose to yield His life rather than commit the sin of pleasing Himself first.

Do we realize what the water and the blood do? There is a twofold cleansing with the water and the blood. We have the inner life that brings us into touch with God, and the outer life that we share with mankind in our relationships. The outer life should be a reflection of Christ's character and attitude from our inner life. God told us to draw near, having our bodies washed with pure water. Jesus came to us by the water and by the blood. He was baptized with water and then shed His blood.

Baptism with water symbolizes the laying aside of sin—washing away the old nature and putting on the new man, yielding the body in total separation from sin. The human work of laying aside sin, as we yield ourselves to God, cannot be separated from the cleansing by Jesus' precious blood. The blood of Jesus was shed with a total sacrifice of "self" on the cross; therefore, it cannot be received without a similar sacrifice of oneself. As we are conformed to His divine nature, Jesus' blood takes us into the death position. The entrance into the full life found in God is obtained by the soul when it is surrendered on the altar of self-sacrifice.

Let's examine whether the unclean can enter into the holy of holies. Can you come into the presence of God in the holy place if you are not cleansed from sin? Has God not given us the power to turn from sin? Is all that we do as a spiritual sacrifice well-pleasing unto God? Ponder these questions as you read on.

Let no one think that the full blessed life is not attainable or too high for one to reach. As we wholly yield ourselves to God, we find the assurance that we can live in complete victory. The individual that truly abandons sin by surrendering the flesh does so by giving himself to the indwelling of Jesus as Lord.

The call to be clean will take us through the veil with Christ by surrendering the flesh. Cleansing cannot take place unless there is an entire separation from everything unclean. God commands His chosen people, "Touch no unclean thing" (2 Cor. 6:17). Separate from the things of the world and the sin that entangles them. Is there a deep yearning within you for more of God? Then separate yourself from that which is unclean, and place yourself daily on the altar of sacrifice.

Jesus chose the cross, taking it up and carrying it daily. Then He finally died upon it. Can we say, "I am crucified with Christ, and my old nature is crucified, for I am dead to sin"? Have we crucified the flesh? The power by which Jesus subdued sin on the cross still lives and works today, and it can work in us as we adopt the crucified life. The blood with which we were purchased, and daily are called to live under, is the blood from the cross. The blood and the cross are united because the blood comes from the cross, leads to the cross, and bears witness to the cross. The power of the cross is found in the precious blood of Jesus, the perfect Lamb of God. Let the words that Jesus repeatedly and boldly declared become your daily vow to God, "Not my will, but Thine be done."

Are you willing to place yourself on the altar and sacrifice your whole self? Are you ready to make the cross your daily dwelling place in fellowship with Jesus? Will you surrender yourself, your will, and all your being, taking up the cross daily and dying to self? We are called to ascend to the altar, laying our lives before Him. We die to self, yet we live for Him to shine through us in all His glory. Dying with Christ leads to a life of perfect love found in the Father. As we lay ourselves upon the altar, as we give ourselves up to the cross and the power of the blood, we become one in faith with Jesus.

Kathryn Kuhlman understood this process of becoming a yielded vessel—she counted herself as nothing. As she stated several times, "It is not golden vessels He asks for. It is not silver vessels. It is yielded vessels. The secret is yield-ness to the Lord."[1] The yielded vessel, empty, has the secret to true life. Once you have experienced yielding your will to the will of the Father, you see it is none of you and all of Him. Allow your entire being to be possessed by God—mind, body, soul, and spirit.

The Holy Spirit will take the yielded and surrendered body and make it the temple of God. The body and life that are surrendered to the Holy Spirit, He will use beyond the human mind's comprehension. Turn yourself completely over to Jesus, and watch what God will do when the Holy Spirit fills your earthen vessel. As the human heart empties itself, it is filled with the Holy Spirit. For we must present our bodies in total sacrifice as yielded vessels for the Holy Spirit to use for the glory of God. Once we surrender our selfish motives and desires, and surrender our will to Him, we truly live to please Him—it is that simple.

I have launched into the living waters of a new way of life in Christ Jesus my Lord. He declares He is coming back for His church, which He described as a bride without spot, wrinkle, or blemish, a glorious church. I have found that the altar of sacrifice, the water of life, and the blood of the cross are what bind me to the taking up of my cross, daily dying to self, and being alive in Him. Let us journey together as we launch into a new way of life.

Chapter 3

GODLESSNESS OR GODLINESS?

I T IS EVIDENT we are living in the Last Days, and darkness has covered the earth. Sin abounds, but the light of Christ shall much more abound. Just as we are concerned as parents about our children's safety in society today, so your heavenly Father is concerned about your spiritual condition. He is coming back for a people who are hot, on fire for Him, and not complacent in their walk with Him. For He wishes we were hot, but because we are lukewarm He will spit us out of His mouth. (See Revelation 3:15.) In His Word, He tells us how we are to live, how to seek Him and find Him, how to abide in His presence, how to cleanse ourselves, and how to die daily to the things of the flesh.

We will cover these areas in His Word together, beginning with the cleansing in the crucified life, into the constant abiding and dwelling in Him, seeking Him through intimate communication and prayer, and then the joy of fellowshiping with Him. This is not a formula, but a way of life in which we say, "*Not my will be done, but the Father's in heaven.*" (See Matthew 26:39.) God is searching for individuals who desire to do His will and who seek Him earnestly. Who is looking to apply for the position of a dead man walking for Christ?

In these Last Days, one can see what 2 Timothy 3:1–5 states will be evident. "But mark this: there will be terrible times in the last days. People will be lovers of themselves, lovers of money, boastful, proud, abusive, disobedient to their parents, ungrateful, unholy, without love, unforgiving, slanderous, without self-control, brutal, not lovers of the good, treacherous, rash, conceited, lovers of pleasure rather than lovers of God—having a form of godliness but denying its power. Have nothing to do with them."

If we break this passage down into smaller phrases, we can see how very strong yet illuminating it is to our hearts and minds. Godlessness consists of many things found in this passage, starting with *lovers of themselves.* This means your desires are first place in your life; you form idols and exalt yourself. To be specific, this means being self-consumed, self-righteous, self-loving, self-pitying, self-confident, self-promoting for the sake of one's ego, and personal glorifying.

The next is *lovers of money,* where the world's riches and the desire for success matter more than God. If obtaining wealth is your priority in life, keep in mind that you cannot love God and money at the same time.

In the last days, people will be *boastful,* full of themselves, bragging, praising, and exalting themselves. The next mark of godlessness usually connects with boastful, and it refers to being *proud,* meaning self-respecting of your status or position in life. Then there is the word *abusive,* which can mean verbal, physical, or even substance abuse. It refers to violating or improperly treating another individual. Abuse is kindled with anger of which one has not taken control and has allowed to become a root in his heart.

Then comes *disobedient to their parents.* As children, we are to have a heart of obedience to our parents. Likewise, as adults we need to be obedient to our heavenly Father. Do not disregard God's commands. Later we will discuss in detail the importance of a heart being obedient.

The seventh portion speaks of being *ungrateful,* not appreciating what God has done for us or given to us, leading to ingratitude. It refers to the receiving of things that God does for us and has done, yet not having a heart of thanksgiving or appreciating Him for His gifts to us.

The next is *unholy,* having no form of holiness dwelling in us that shows outward to others. An unholy man does not walk with God, but a holy man does walk with God. Being holy requires a purification of the heart, a heart that is undivided. The holy heart is fully given up to God. This person lives a holy life day after day.

Then comes *without love.* This individual is self-seeking and does not delight in the goodwill of mankind. God calls us to be loving, kind, and giving to our fellow man, because His greatest gift is love. To be without love, one is not devoted fully to God, for He is love. (See 1 John 4:7–8.)

In the rest of the passage, there is *unforgiving,* which is to hold resentment in one's heart, to not excuse, or to retain anger against another individual. Then there is the word *slanderous,* referring to purposely speaking badly about another or putting them down; malicious gossip. The next is *without self-control,* to not control the evil thoughts or desires of your heart and mind. This is not crucifying the flesh and not submitting your will to God's will. Then comes *brutal,* to be cruel in words, actions, or deeds to others; to show negative attitudes unbecomingly. To become *not lovers of good* means one is a lover of what is not pure, holy, or of God. To be opposite what is good is to be a lover of what is evil or bad. *Treacherous* is a person who is a deceiver or who violates his allegiance to God.

Beware of Satan, who is called the deceiver who violated his allegiance to God. Satan's plan is to deceive God's people. The individual who is *rash* is quick or hasty in their attitudes, and takes no time to reflect on what the Lord may be revealing to him. The *conceited* individual likes to exalt himself above God and others. He displays excessive pride because he is too highly minded of himself. The next are *lovers of pleasure rather than lovers of God*. This is when the things of this world and the pleasures thereof are put before God. Self is first, so your god is you. The last passage is *having a form of godliness but denying its power* to transform you. It is merely a mask one wears on special days or events to impress others, or a label to verify position in life.

God is calling His people to cleanse themselves from all manner of evil and sin; a transformation of the heart is necessary. In Mark 10:19, God says, "You know the commandments: 'do not murder, do not commit adultery, do not steal, do not give false testimony, do not defraud, honor your father and mother.'" God prohibits wrong motives, actions, and attitudes against yourself and your fellow man. Our requirement is to be purified and surrendered to His perfect will and plan for our lives.

God desires to make things new for us. He calls us to live or abide in the crucified life with Christ. When we read the Ten Commandments and refuse to obey, we pay a price. Sin has a way of appearing harmless at first. The beginnings of sin appear rather innocent and sound rather reasonable. Satan does not burst upon us with a grand formal attack—he is crafty and quite subtle; he disguises himself well. Though sin appears innocent at first, one becomes ensnared in the net of deception.

Satan operates in a totally different sphere than God. The enemy never operates in truth. Satan's nature is deception, and the world today is filled with great deception. The deceiving of man's mind is where Satan operates. God sent His Son Jesus, who is the only way, truth, and life. (See John 14:6.)

In Revelation 21:5–8, the Word says, "He who was seated on the throne said, 'I am making everything new!' Then he said, 'Write this down, for these words are trustworthy and true.' He said to me: 'It is done. I am the Alpha and the Omega, the Beginning and the End. To him who is thirsty I will give to drink without cost from the spring of the water of life. He who overcomes will inherit all this, and I will be his God and he will be my son. But the cowardly, the unbelieving, the vile, the murderers, the sexually immoral, those who practice magic arts, the idolaters and all liars—there place will be in the fiery lake of burning sulfur. This is the second death.'"

God is explicit here on what to do and not do. A godly man of character will cleanse himself, or crucify the flesh from all manner of evil, and pursue righteousness, faith, hope, love, and peace. When a man of God cleanses himself continually, he becomes an instrument for godly purposes, made holy for the Master's use. Note that when men or women of God cleanse themselves continually (being daily crucified with Christ), they become obedient to God. Those who do not obey will have their place in the lake of fire—hell. In 2 Timothy 2:21 it says, "If a man cleanses himself from the latter, he will be an instrument for noble purposes, made holy, useful for the Master and prepared to do any good work." When we seek God with all our heart, there burns within us a desire to walk in obedience to Him. We become willing to lay our lives down for Him on the altar of sacrifice. True believers delight themselves in the Lord by living a life of obedience. Hear the voice of God calling—who will become as a dead man walking?

To not please God, to grieve His heart, will lead to grieving in your own heart. Where God's Spirit is grieved, He will not stay. The choice is ours to serve self or God—godless living or godly living. Psalm 4:3 says, "Know that the LORD has set apart the godly for himself; the LORD will hear when I call to him."

In 1 Peter 1:13–16, "Therefore, prepare your minds for

action; be self-controlled; set your hope fully on the grace to be given you when Jesus Christ is revealed. As obedient children, do not conform to the evil desires you had when you lived in ignorance. But just as he who called you is holy, so be holy in all you do; for it is written: 'Be holy, because I am holy.'" Called to be holy—this is a command from God. When He tells us to be holy, He is instructing us how we are to live. Your entire being is to be possessed by God. What portions of your life are a hindrance in your walk with God? Whatever they are, only a complete surrender to the Lord can set you free. In every relationship of life, home, business, or church, give yourself totally to the guidance of the Spirit of God.

There is a difference between true believers and those who claim to believe but show no fruit of abiding in Christ. An individual is recognized by the fruit of abiding in Christ Jesus. Those who abide in Him bear the fruit in their lives, those who do not display the evidence of not abiding in Him. The fruit bearer's agenda is total obedience to the will of the Father. The non-fruit bearer is in search of what they can get or how to benefit themselves.

Be watchful, and pray that you remain submitted to God. It is a place of abiding and living in the Lord. We can liken it to the fact that we do not refuse our bodies sleep, water, or food. They are essential for life, but much more important is time spent with God. Remember, as Jesus walked upon the face of the earth, He set aside a portion of His day for the Father, always doing the Father's will. So must we set aside that time of communicating with our Father, then listening to Him and doing His will.

> Lord God, let it be my prayer today to be holy, I repent
> of all the sins I have committed. Come to me, Lord, and
> shine Your light upon my heart, revealing those things that
> I must die to so Christ's light can go forth and change, not
> only me, but also those You place within my path. God,

ignite within me Your holy passion for Your people. I praise Your holy name, Lord, as today is a new day and a new beginning for me. Amen.

Ephesians 5:26–27, 32 says, "To make her holy, cleansing her by the washing with water through the word, and to present her to himself as a radiant church, without stain or wrinkle or any other blemish, but holy and blameless.... This is a profound mystery—but I am talking about Christ and the church [his bride]." We cleanse ourselves through the Word of God and by surrendering ourselves completely to His perfect will. We are to live life daily humbling ourselves to the Lord's will, and dying to self, which involves crucifying the flesh each day so God has control in our lives. Determine to be the radiant church for which He will return.

Be ready! Embark upon the blessedness of a life completely transformed and made clean by the blood of Jesus. A life full of zeal, love, joy, faith, and power—all for the work of the Lord. Our entire being—mind, body, soul, and spirit—in complete surrender as a sacrifice to God. Isaiah 52:1–2 reads, "Awake, awake [*pray now*], O Zion, clothe yourself with strength [*you clothe yourself with the garments of splendor and strength from His Word*]. Put on your garments of splendor, O Jerusalem, the holy city. The uncircumcised and defiled will not enter you again. [*Leave the old self behind, never to come back to that old self nature again, and then the evil one Satan who defiles cannot come into you again.*] Shake off your dust [*all the dirt of your past life and enter into the new life reigning and abiding with Christ*]; rise up, sit enthroned, O Jerusalem. Free yourself [*you have the ability to decide to be bound or freed, it is your choice*] from the chains on your neck, O captive Daughter of Zion."

True repentance is a turning away from sin. The heart, body, mind, soul, and spirit unite in following only God and His commands. Repentance results from a transformation of one's life from within the individual. He or she becomes more Christlike. He is crucified with Him to sin and all its evil desires. The transformation is evident to others around him, for he begins to reflect Christ. The individual who has turned from all manner of sin is crucified daily. He seeks God's face, and can count himself dead to sin, but alive unto God.

Does God really own you? Are you sealed with His love and marked as His child? Have you laid yourself on the altar of sacrifice—giving up self, allowing the water to wash over you, and letting the blood cleanse you from sin?

Chapter 4

DEAD TO SIN—ALIVE TO GOD

ROMANS 6:8-14 SAYS, "Now if we died with Christ, we believe that we will also live with him. For we know that since Christ was raised from the dead, he cannot die again; death no longer has mastery over him. The death he died, he died to sin once for all; but the life he lives, he lives to God. In the same way, count yourselves dead to sin [*as Christ did*] but alive to God in Christ Jesus. Therefore do not let sin reign in your mortal body so that you obey its evil desires. Do not offer the parts of your body to sin, as instruments of wickedness, but rather offer yourselves to God, as those who have been brought from death to life; and offer the parts of your body to him as instruments of righteousness. For sin shall not be your master, because you are not under law, but under grace [*Christ's empowerment of the cross*]."

Let's clarify grace and law and the commands of God. Sin

is a power that enslaves you to the evil desires of this world, and your master is the devil. When Scripture states "not under law," it refers to the Old Testament law, which did not enable us to resist the power of sin. Jesus paid the price for our sins through His death and resurrection. Because of the grace (divine assistance) of God, we now can resist the power of the evil one. The choice is ours whether we resist the evil one and choose God as our master. This does not give us the right to go about and sin just because we believe we are forgiven, and therefore not liable for ourselves. None of us shall escape judgment for the way we choose to live.

There has been erroneous teaching on this, and later in this chapter we will cover this ground. The body's lure to self-pleasing has seduced the soul and pulled the spirit of man down into servitude. Satan came to impart the poison of pride into Eve's ears, and Adam quickly followed. Since that moment, mankind has listened to the spew of poison from Satan and embraced the idols of selfishness. The "I" idol, self-seeking and self-pleasing—"I" am first—comes from the place where all sin originates, which is from Satan. (See Isaiah 14:12–15.)

In Romans 6:15–18 we read, "What then? Shall we sin because we are not under law but under grace? By no means! [*This says no emphatically.*] Don't you know that when you offer yourselves to someone to obey him as slaves, you are slaves to the one whom you obey—whether you are slaves to sin, which leads to death, or to obedience, which leads to righteousness? But thanks be to God that, though you used to be slaves to sin, you wholeheartedly obeyed the form of teaching to which you were entrusted. You have been set free from sin and have become slaves to righteousness." For God gave every man a free will and the ability to decide for himself to whom he will submit and serve.

Christian obedience cannot be forced, but must come from a willing heart ready to obey. It is where we turn our hearts to God, surrender to His commands, and decide to obey the voice of the Father above all else. Our body, soul, and spirit must become a living sacrifice to God with His Holy Spirit dwelling in us. There we will find a sweet fellowship with Him.

Many prefer to veer away from complete surrender to God and go about living as they want, not as the Lord would command. Romans 8:12–14 speaks of an obligation we have as Christians: "Therefore, brothers, we have an obligation—but it is not to the sinful nature, to live according to it. For if you live according to the sinful nature, you will die; but if by the spirit you put to death the misdeeds of the body, you will live, because those who are led by the Spirit of God are sons of God." Your obligation is to put to death the misdeeds of the body, by the Holy Spirit. The choice is yours—decide whether you will surrender your life and heart to live a life free from the sinful nature.

When a person dies on earth, he no longer has any desire for earthly things. So it can be likened to a man who has died to the attractions of sin: he has no desire or need for what sin would offer; in fact he hates sin. Christians who are alive unto God offer themselves to God 100 percent. They have made their life a never-ending offering to God, to work for Him while giving all the glory only to God. In Romans 12:1–2 the apostle Paul writes, "Therefore, I urge you, brothers, in view of God's mercy, to offer your bodies as living sacrifices, holy and pleasing to God—this is your spiritual act of worship. Do not conform any longer to the pattern of this world, but be transformed by the renewing of your mind. Then you will be able to test and approve what God's will is—his good, pleasing and perfect will." This says to offer your bodies as living sacrifices, not the ritual activity, but an actual dedication of oneself with the heart, mind, and will, in a totally surrendered state, to the Lord. It is simply the crucified life of dying to self and reigning with Christ.

The dedicated Christian agonizes over the thought of committing any sin, and it drives him to stay purified within his heart. Sin, to the dedicated man, is like poison to his very soul. If we grieve the Lord God's heart, may it be our prayer that by His Holy Spirit He grieves our hearts likewise.

The Holy Spirit is not a person or power for us to use as we see fit. One of the greatest lessons each of us can learn is how to yield completely to the Holy Spirit. He requires a yielded, empty vessel, and it is this vessel that He uses to perform His mighty work. God calls for the individual to surrender all, where the soul is wholly committed to pleasing God and doing His divine will.

When two people marry and make vows to each other, they are entering into a faithful marriage covenant. They have set their hearts and minds on being devoted only to each other. They have said, in essence, "Another shall not interest me because you are my true love and my heart is fixed to living with you."

God calls those people who are His and serve Him, "the bride of Christ." The bride is to make a commitment to her Bridegroom; this is a covenant vow. John 3:29–30 says, "The bride belongs to the bridegroom. The friend who attends the bridegroom waits and listens for him, and is full of joy when he hears the bridegroom's voice. That joy is mine, and is now complete. He must become greater; I must become less." When the bride (church) devotes her heart to the Bridegroom (Jesus), her commitment is, "I trust in Him." So she counts her life as being devoted to the Bridegroom (Jesus), and her eyes do not wander to idols.

The desire within you should be only for Jesus, and you cannot think of yielding to sin's seductions and lures any longer. The position you would take is, "I will have nothing to do with yielding to sin, for my mind and heart are forever settled on Christ Jesus."

The wondrous works of the Lord and the inspired Word of God cause the Christian to seek freedom from sin more than he or she seeks being saved from hell. When you seek to live a life free from sin, the benefit is being saved from hell and spending eternity in heaven. Seek what is true and what is of God; be fully devoted to Him and hate sin. Become dead to sin and alive unto God.

True sacrifice is a voluntary act, to give up something in exchange for a more pressing desire within your being. When you sacrifice your life to God, you give up yourself in exchange for the perfect will of God. The life of a Christian is surrender—a giving up of yourself to God and changing your will and desire to His perfect will and desire for your life.

Let's look at it this way. How would you like to wear the same clothes day in and day out, never washing or being clean? The Christian is called to put off, cast away, cleanse, and renounce his former way of life, and put on the garment of the bride that is pure white and clean. Ephesians 4:22–24 says, "You were taught, with regard to your former way of life, to put off your old self, which is being corrupted by its deceitful desires; to be made new in the attitude of your minds; and to put on the new self, created to be like God in true righteousness and holiness." We are created to be like God, not like the world. We put on the new and leave the old behind—we dress ourselves with the proper godly garment. So Colossians 3:9–10 tells us, "Do not lie to each other, since you have taken off your old self with its practices and have put on the new self, which is being renewed in knowledge in the image of its Creator." This means you decide if you will live in accordance with God's kingdom rules and commands. Your desire should be to reflect the image of your creator, His image only—choose your garment wisely.

Denying self, taking up the cross of death to self, is the key to being His disciple and being counted as worthy of Christ. Galatians 2:20 states, "I have been crucified with Christ and I no longer live, but Christ lives in me. The life I live in the body, I live by faith in the Son of God, who loved me and gave himself for me." Crucified with Christ, dead to sin and the power it once held, you are then no longer living for self as Christ lives in you and you live by faith in the Son. Romans 6:5–7, 11–12 tells us, "If we have been united with him like this in his death, we will certainly also be united with him in his resurrection. For we know that our old self was crucified with Him so that the body of sin might be done away with, that we should no longer be slaves to sin—because anyone who has died has been freed from sin.... In the same way, count yourselves dead to sin but alive to God in Christ Jesus. Therefore do not let sin reign in your mortal body so that you obey its evil desires." The fleshly nature of sin is to be dead in you, no longer ruling in your body for you have died to sinful living. Considering Matthew 10:38, 16:24, and Luke 14:27, we find these words of Jesus repeated three times, ending differently in each verse, but with the same message of denying self. Matthew 16:24 says, "If anyone would come after me, he must deny himself and take up his cross and follow me." Matthew 10:38 says, "Not worthy of me." So the message is if you do not take His cross and follow Him, you are not worthy of Him. Luke 14:27 says, "Cannot be my disciple." Take up the cross of Christ and crucify your flesh, for this is the key to being counted a disciple worthy of Christ. It is part of the Christian's call to service, to die to self in order to be transformed into the divine character of Christ—to be an imitator of His divine nature. The cross identifies that the believing disciple or Christian is now crucified, united with Christ as one.

When one seeks intimacy with Christ, or to know Him and reflect Him, the secret lies in uniting with Him on the cross, living the crucified life. The process of crucifying flesh is painful, and most shrink from the suffering and death associated with it. As we press in, pursuing Christ, and cry out to our Father to reveal His divine will and plan for us, He supplies the strength to proceed to death to self. Kathryn Kuhlman stated, "I die a thousand deaths before I ever walk out on the platform or stage, because I know how ordinary I am. I know that I have nothing."[1] When you take up that cross, you take up the sign of death to self. The greatest hour of your life will be the hour you take up the cross and die to self.

Christ prayed in the garden for God's will only, before He went to the cross to be crucified. Christ was crucifying anything that might have hindered the call and purpose to which He was born. Christ was already dead to self. Those He interceded for then, and for whom He now intercedes, are you and me. We are crucified with Him, because He took us all to the cross with Him. Remaining dead to self (*crucified*) is a choice we make. To become partakers of Christ, we need to embrace the crucified life of death to self—abiding, living, dwelling, and surrendering all of ourselves to Him totally.

The apostle Paul writes in Galatians 2:20, "I have been crucified with Christ and I no longer live [*he had death to self reigning in Him*], but Christ lives in me." *Christ has made residence in me* was what Paul was saying; *He dwells and lives in me and I in Him.* Those who belong to Christ live life not as their own, for they have chosen the crucified life—death to self. Read Galatians 5:24 and 6:14: "Those who belong to Christ Jesus have crucified the sinful nature with its passions and desires." (*Who belongs to Christ, those who are crucified?*) "May I never boast except in the cross of our Lord Jesus Christ, through which the world has been crucified to me, and I to the world." Partaking in the crucified life with Christ, I now have crucified my life of self and the desires of this world. I have crucified the desires of my selfish life to be a partner with Christ in a life of victory.

Do not let yourself come down off the cross. Every moment the flesh needs to be submitted and surrendered up to the cross. When the Scripture says the old man or old nature of living in sin was crucified, it means the man who knew not God came to God, for he desired to be crucified (*dead to self*) with Christ. The flesh nature, or human nature, needs to be crucified daily.

To be crucified with Christ gives us freedom from the

29

power of sin—that is why staying crucified enables us to stay free from sin. The deeper the cross is within you, the brighter Christ shines within you. Always beware that the old fleshly nature will seek to deceive you that living this life of crucifixion—death to self—is just expecting too much. Your only way to stay in the crucified life is with constant abiding fellowship with Christ. Remember that "crucified with Christ Jesus" means freed from the power of sin.

It is when we come down off the cross of submission and death to self that our problems begin. The Holy Spirit has been assigned to comfort you, to reveal truth to you, to glorify Christ in you, and to guide you. The Holy Spirit will be more valuable to you when you regard Him as a dear beloved friend who is interested in transforming you into an imitator of Christ.

The cross of Jesus Christ was for us, for in it we find the path to living life in Christ. The power of the cross destroys sin and death, and keeps us in the power of eternal life with Christ. When we have complete faith in the power of the cross we gladly take the cross along with its pain, suffering with its blessed victories.

A PRAYER OF SURRENDER—DYING TO SELF

Lord Jesus my Savior, I come before You and humbly ask that You by Your Holy Spirit reveal to me the hidden glory of the unity of being crucified with You. Lord Jesus, You came to earth and took my place on the cross, so that I may now share with You the joys of the crucified life. You call me, Lord, to follow You, to take up my cross and follow You, and to be like You. Lord, may Your Holy Spirit reveal to me the full power of the crucified life in Christ. Lord, I can only overcome the power of sin and its evil desires when I yield myself entirely to You. To abide in You and stay in the position of crucifying the flesh is my desire, precious Lord. O Lamb of God, sweet Lamb of God, it is You whom I seek, and in You whom I have all hope and faith.

*In You may I always live, yielded and surrendered to do
Your will. Amen.*

When we examine the life of Christ as our example, we
see that He did not come to please Himself. We see Him as
the exact opposite of one who would live to please himself.
It gives us hope and faith that in the abiding, dwelling fellowship of the crucified life, one is found to be dead to sin
and self. Through the crucified Christ, we receive the divine
power to no longer please our old nature or flesh, but to deny
self. Denying self was the entire domain of Christ's life, and
those who wish to follow Him and be His disciple must deny
themselves. In Matthew 16:24, Jesus said to His disciples, "If
anyone would come after me, he must deny himself and take
up his cross and follow me."

When you want to be like Christ, there are commands you
must obey. The first is denying self and taking up His cross—
crucifying the flesh and the desires thereof. Then, follow Him
and take on His character. Do not be afraid of the death-to-
self application by crucifying this old nature. That is how His
divine nature is imparted to us.

How often have we defeated His plan for us? We have all
been guilty of obstructing Him some time during our lives.
I have been guilty more than once because of my selfish little
sins of destruction. Sin left un-repented can cause damage to
the body as God's temple. Like a termite, it will eat away until
finally the building is destroyed and tumbles to the ground.
Just as termites bring down the building, so sin eats away at
your heart and destroys the purpose of your life. Do not allow
Satan to rob you of something that you could have done, or
could be doing, for the kingdom of God.

Chapter 5

KEYS TO GOD'S HOUSE

T HE KEYS TO God's kingdom are available to you. Jesus revealed the keys when Peter acknowledged Him as "the Christ, the son of the living God" (Matt. 16:16). Then Jesus told Peter this was not made known to Him by man, "…but by my Father in heaven" (v. 17). Jesus then informed Peter that on the Rock (*of Jesus Christ*), "I will build my church, and the gates of Hades will not overcome it" (v. 18). Jesus went on to say, "I will give you the keys of the kingdom of heaven" (v. 19). These keys unlock that which once legally bound you. Therefore, whatever you bind (*in Jesus' name and authority*) on earth will be legally bound in heaven. The second key will loose on earth that which held you as God's Word is loosing it in heaven. Two keys are listed here—one to legally bind the enemy and another to loose you from what once held you in bondage. (See Matthew 16:19.)

Keys unlock and allow entrance through a specific portal. Jesus possesses the keys to life. The first key is acknowledging that you will lay yourself down on the altar of complete sacrifice—making a binding agreement with God, giving your all to Him. The second key is the blood of Jesus that loosens the power of Satan over your life as you remain crucified with Christ.

The keys to the kingdom are available for you, but the choice is yours. Now, once you have committed yourself to Christ, completely acknowledging Him as your Lord and Savior, Christ says, "Here are the keys to My Father's house." God knows the enemy, and He knows you need the keys to His house. For the enemy will target you because you choose Christ and His kingdom. Satan tempts everyone; even Jesus Himself was tempted in the desert. Since our Father God knows Satan's plans, He says to His people, "I give you the keys to My house." First, you abide in Him, then He promises to abide in you, setting you free from the power of the enemy.

Christ tells us, "Entrance is granted only to those who live in Me and I in them" (John 15:4, author's paraphrase). As God's children, we have access to the kingdom of God, using these keys and His Word. The keys given to you have power to bind things that do not line up with God, and then loose those things that have kept you bound. As you have examined yourself, have you found parts of your life that you just have not surrendered or are struggling with? The next few chapters are going to take you through the key steps to be cleansed, along with surrendering your will to the will of the Father. The keys are given as a promise to the individual who has chosen Christ as his or her Rock of salvation. The church, God's people, receives these keys to defeat the enemy that tries to come against them. To be able to use the keys, one has to be a part of God's family—God does not give you the keys to His house unless you are His. We then may ask, "How do we get free from the enemy?" Submit to God by giving yourself completely to Him; accept Christ as your Lord. That is the only way to receive the keys to the Father's house and to defeat the enemy when he comes to tempt you or destroy you. Pray this prayer of salvation if you do not have Christ living in you. It is time to lay yourself on the altar of sacrifice:

Jesus, I acknowledge You as the holy Lamb of God, who came to die for my sins, so that I may have eternal life with You. I know I must come as a little child, humbly asking for forgiveness of all my sins, and accept You as Lord of my life. Jesus, come, as I surrender my life to You on the altar of sacrifice; be the Lord over my life. Thank You, Jesus, for dying for me and showing me the way. Thank You, God, for giving to me the precious gift of salvation. In Jesus' name I pray, amen.

As we walk through the following simple prayer on binding and loosing, examine what it is in your life that needs to be bound and loosed. You may also want to go to the first chapter and review 2 Timothy 3:1–5 once again.

A Prayer of Binding and Loosing

Father, I thank You for Your Word that is unchangeable, and I thank You that You are always the same. I thank You, Lord, for imparting to me Your divine wisdom and illuminating me. I humbly ask, Lord, that by Your Spirit You reveal to me the true condition of my way of living. God, reveal those things that need to be removed from my life today. I bind, in the name of Jesus, all anger, fear, bitterness, unforgivingness, self-centeredness, and all idols in my life that exalt themselves above You. I bind them now, in Jesus' name. Your Word states whatever I bind on earth is bound in heaven (love of money, boastfulness, pride, abusiveness, disobedience, ungratefulness, un-holiness, unloving, slanderous words and actions, brutality, conceitedness, rashness, treacherousness, loving things of the

world, religious spirits, lying, murmuring, sexual immo-
rality, magic arts and witchcraft, and idolatry). I loose, by
the power of the blood, all evil thoughts the enemy has
tried to establish in my mind, will, and emotions that have
exalted themselves above You, God. I bind my mind to
the mind of Christ and loose those thought patterns that
have tried to prohibit me from walking according to Your
divine will in my life. Lord, I choose to cleanse my heart
of all impurities and stand in obedience to Your Word. I
will choose today to turn from all my wicked ways, and set
my mind, heart, will, and emotions to serving You alone,
Lord. I thank You for the keys to the kingdom, and for the
power of the blood to bind and loose those things in my life
that need to be removed. Thank You, Lord. Amen.

You may be thinking at this point, *How do I know when my soul is surrendered?* Remember we die daily, and each new day brings new battles with new trials and tribulations. This is not meant to discourage you. For there is a place where you will come into rest, knowing that things do not affect you because Christ is in control when you surrender your soul to Him. When you realize it is time for you to use the keys to the Father's house, use them. Perseverance pays, so continue in your commitment to Christ. God knows if your heart is set on running the great race set before you.

Second Corinthians 10:3–5 says, "For though we live in the world, we do not wage war as the world does. The weapons we fight with are not the weapons of the world. On the contrary, they have divine power to demolish strongholds. We demolish arguments and every pretension that sets itself up against the knowledge of God, and we take captive every thought to make it obedient to Christ." Every thought should be taken captive or tied up (this *is binding*) to make it subject and obedient to Christ. We take those thoughts captive, tie them up, bind them, and loose ourselves to God's will so we can walk in obedience to God. We demolish all thoughts, arguments, and self-ordained ideas that may exalt themselves against God. But beware—a kingdom or individual divided cannot stand with God and with himself.

In Matthew 12:25–29, "Jesus knew their thoughts and said to them, 'Every kingdom divided against itself will be ruined, and every city or household divided against itself will not stand. If Satan drives out Satan, he is divided against himself. How then can his kingdom stand? And if I drive out demons by Beelzebub, by whom do your people drive them out? So then, they will be your judges. But if I drive out demons by the Spirit of God, then the kingdom of God has come upon you. Or again, how can anyone enter a strong man's house and carry off his possessions unless he first ties up the strong man? [*Possesses the Father's Key.*] Then he can rob his house." This refers to the first key of the kingdom being used to bind the strong man. If Satan drives out Satan, he is divided against himself. This tells us that Satan cannot drive out himself for he will not divide his kingdom. Just as God cannot divide His kingdom or His keys, rules, or commands, neither does Satan divide his kingdom.

The power and fullness of God is not seen as it should be seen because the bride needs to get her house cleaned and put in order.

Believer, come bathe in the river of life; plunge into the water and experience its cleansing. Surrender in faith to the river of life flowing from heaven to you right now. It is the blessed Spirit of God flowing like a rushing river as you place yourself in it. The Spirit of God calls you to let the waters rush over your soul to cleanse, heal, and purify. As you yield, a mighty rushing of cleansing water washes over you—it is the power of the Holy Spirit. As you submit, He reveals the areas of your life that need the stain of sin removed. First comes the man submitting himself on the altar, then the Holy Spirit reveals the sins that have stained the individual, holding him in chains of bondage. Remember the altar is where the Lamb of God was sacrificed as the great sin offering once and forever. The altar is also where we must present ourselves as a living sacrifice yielded to God.

Submitting to God, hearing His voice, and obeying it are necessary steps we all must embrace. Continue to feed your spirit and grow stronger each day with God. Be ever changing, growing, and maturing. For you can spend your entire life serving God, communicating with Him, searching His Word, and never know all His facets. Strive to know more of Him, and dig deep as you grow daily in Him.

Living as sacrifices to God is defined in Romans 12:1-2: "Therefore, I urge you, brothers, in view of God's mercy, to offer your bodies as living sacrifices, holy and pleasing to God—this is your spiritual act of worship. Do not conform any longer to the pattern of this world, but be transformed by the renewing of your mind. Then you will be able to test and approve what God's will is—his good, pleasing and perfect will." Walk in the perfect will of God, and offer yourselves as living sacrifices to live holy and pure lives.

Once you have cleansed yourself and obtained the keys to binding and loosing, guard yourself well, because the thief will try to come and steal what has been deposited. Do not return to the pattern of living in what the world offers; instead renew your way of living by obeying God's Word. Keep in mind, God is with you at all times. Do not grieve His Spirit. Ask yourself, "Is Christ grieving over my lack of wholeheartedness to Him?"

The Scripture tells us how to guard His Word, which has been deposited in us. Proverbs 4:13, 20–27 tells us, "Hold on to instruction, do not let it go; guard it well, for it is your life.... My son, pay attention to what I say; listen closely to my words. Do not let them out of your sight, keep them within your heart; for they are life to those who find them and health to a man's whole body. Above all else, guard your heart, for it is the wellspring of life. Put away perversity from your mouth; keep corrupt talk far from your lips. Let your eyes look straight ahead, fix your gaze directly before you. Make level paths for your feet and take only ways that are firm. Do not swerve to the right or the left; keep your foot from evil." We are supposed to remove all moral hindrances and keep our hearts fixed and guarded, obeying all instructions and commands from God. We are instructed to not let God's Word go, but to guard it, to keep it before our eyes, and to keep it within our hearts. Those who do this are counted as dead men walking for Christ. In Proverbs 7:2–3 we read, "Keep my commands and you will live; guard my teachings as the apple of your eye. Bind them on your fingers; write them on the tablet of your heart." Proverbs 19:16 says, "He who obeys instructions guards his life, but he who is contemptuous [*disobedient*] of his ways will die." The choice comes back to us. We have a free will to choose the life of obedience to the Master with the keys to His house, or not. *What do we truly want? Do we want to lay ourselves at the Savior's feet on the altar of sacrifice? Have we surrendered to the power of the cross saying, "Not my will, but Thine be done, Father"?*

Chapter 6

IGNITED PASSION THROUGH INTIMACY

W HO WERE THE men of passion? Who will be the next people of passion willing to pursue Christ? Is it your desire to be a person of passion, seeking and pursing the Lord? Hebrews 11 lists some people who passionately pursued the Lord. They lived by faith, with a heart that always pursued God. Abel offered a better sacrifice to God and was commended as a righteous man. God spoke well of Abel's offerings. Enoch was taken from this life and never experienced death. But before he was taken, he was commended as one who pleased God. Noah had faith and a holy fear, building the ark to save his family.

Abraham obeyed and went to the land where he would receive his inheritance. Isaac and Jacob were heirs with Abraham of this same promise of inheritance. Abraham became known as the father of many nations because God considered him faithful. All these people were living by faith when they died. *(They persevered and never quit. They were determined that they would complete the task and obey the voice of God.)* Moses persevered because he saw the Lord who is invisible. Moses had a deep desire to know God and to be led only by Him. The Lord passed by Moses, and afterward Moses was a man of ignited passion.

The Bible is full of men and women who obeyed God and had faith in Him. Hear God calling now—who will burn with the fire of God and have a passion to follow Him? God is a consuming fire and desires for us to yield ourselves totally to Him. Let it be our prayer, "O God, that we are consumed by Your holy fire. Let it burn in us, out of us, and into all the world so others will see You. Lord, let Your Word be fire within our entire being—spirit, soul, and body. Let Your fire, Father, consume us and overtake us in Jesus' name." This world will only be changed when people see Jesus living and moving through His people, as imitators of Christ.

> Then those who feared the LORD talked with each other, and the LORD listened and heard. A scroll of remembrance was written in his presence concerning those who feared the LORD and honored his name. "They will be mine," says the LORD Almighty, "in the day when I make up my treasured possession. I will spare them, just as in compassion a man spares his son who serves him. And you will again see the distinction between the righteous and the wicked, between those who serve God and those who do not."
>
> —MALACHI 3:16–18

The Lord hears those who fear Him, live by faith, and serve Him. A scroll (book) of remembrance contains the names of those who fear and honor Him. They are His people, devoted to God alone, who live with a passion to serve Him only. Hebrews

11 tells us that these people of passion served the Lord, so their names are forever recorded in His scroll of remembrance.

How will the Lord remember you? Will it be as a man or woman of great faith, obedient to the Master as one who lays down his life for Christ? We either belong to Christ, or we oppose Him. Whom do you serve? There are those who received Christ as their Savior, yet deep within their souls stirs the longing to pursue Him and to know Him intimately. They are passionate in their pursuit, and they shall find Him.

Is there a fire that burns within you for more of God? When the apostle Paul wrote, "I die every day," he was saying, "I crucify this flesh anew every day as I enter into the presence of God." (See 1 Corinthians 15:31.) God is trying to prepare His people for the Last Days in which we presently live. If we turn our hearts to God and His true holiness, we will receive a great outpouring of His glory as promised in His Word. The choice is ours whether we yield our lives to the Great Master or another. Jesus repeatedly warned His disciples that He was to be crucified and that they also must bear their cross. Jesus was speaking of denying the innerman, losing the self life, and embracing the fellowship of the cross. The apostle Paul stated, "Those who belong to Christ Jesus have crucified the sinful nature with its passions and desires" (Gal. 5:24). We so often rejoice that Christ died for us, but then do not rejoice when we are called to take up our cross. In faith, offer your entire being to God. Choose the crucified life, reflect it to others, and preach it to the world.

Kathryn Kuhlman said many times that she died a thousand deaths, before she could come out on stage to minister to God's people.[1] She knew the crucified life, reflected it, and preached it. People with ignited passions for the Master, whose hearts follow after Him, become as dead men walking. The question is, who is willing to die to self and become a dead man walking for the Lord? Read 2 Corinthians 6:16–7:1: "What agreement is there between the temple of God and idols? For we are the temple of the living God. As God has said: 'I will live with them and walk among them, and I will be their God, and they will be my people.' 'Therefore come out from them and be separate, says the Lord. Touch no unclean thing and I will receive you.' 'I will be a Father to you, and you will be my sons and daughters, says the Lord Almighty.' Since we have these promises, dear friends, let us purify ourselves from everything that contaminates body and spirit, perfecting holiness out of reverence for God."

There is no agreement between the temple of God and idols. If you are in Christ, you separate yourself from the things of the world. There burns within you a desire to be pure and holy, for the same reason you came to Christ. He loved you with a love like no other. His love is a perfect love, beyond all human love. Christ died for you when you never even knew Him. This gift, that He gives to those who come to Him as their Savior *(Lord: supreme authority over another)* is the perfect gift. So in light of the perfect gift of love and salvation, we should desire Him above all earthly things. The soul should long for Him more than anything else. Experiencing this perfect love should cause a deep desire to seek Him, pursue Him, and walk with Him daily to burn within you.

Christ is coming back soon. The body of Christ needs to get ready today! No longer is it time to play church and try to satisfy man or those of authority in the church. God never called His bride or church to be men-pleasers; He called His bride to obey Him and His Word. Believers are commanded to have no other gods before Him. God is coming back for a bride without spot, wrinkle, or blemish.

There is no use waiting for God to change your will or heart. He gave you free will and a heart to choose Him. He waits to see who will choose Him, obey His commands, and follow Him. So where is the bride of Christ, and who is she really following after? The army of the Lord must be ready. We need to get ourselves in order. The bride is the army, and she has to be dressed for battle. The army must walk by faith in the power of the Holy Spirit and be fully committed to the Lord. He will not take a lukewarm church that is self-seeking. Revelation 3:15–16 says, "I know your deeds, that you are neither cold nor hot. I wish you were either one or the other! So, because you are lukewarm—neither hot nor cold—I am about to spit you out of my mouth." God is saying, "I will eject you from Me, no longer in Me or part of Me."

Who are the ones that could be considered the lukewarm? Those who are pleasing self first; their god is themselves along with their own desires. They are not surrendered to God. They have no alliance, loyalty, or union with Him. Remember that God is a jealous God, and He will have no other gods before Him.

It is time for the church to measure up to the standards of the Lord, not to the world and man. It takes a persevering spirit to rise above the status quo that exists in many churches today. The church must arise and cease from the slumbering state she has allowed to take hold. The church needs to follow the Holy Spirit. The winds of change have already started blowing across this world. God is going to break forth in the lives of those who seek Him with all their heart. The psalmist describes it this way: "As the deer pants for streams of water, so my soul pants for you, O God, My soul thirsts for God, for the living God" (Ps. 42:1–2). Is your soul thirsty for God?

The Holy Trinity, God, Jesus, and the Holy Spirit, are all living beings. They have the capability to communicate with us through our spirits and within our minds, our emotions, and wills. We cannot see the Holy Trinity, yet we know them if we abide in them in a deep personal relationship. When we pursue the lover of our soul, we seek Him to know Him more intimately. It burns within us to be like Him. It is possible to arrive at the place where nothing else matters but being like Him and being transformed into an imitator of His divine nature. Beware that you do not insist upon trying to adjust Christ's image and character closer to your own image. Stay in the crucified life, but live as Christ lives. When pursuing Christ with a passion to know Him, the flesh is cut away more and more, and the divine character of Christ starts to shine through.

When your sole purpose and soul desire become knowing Christ, pleasing God, and doing the will of the Father, you become as a dead man walking for Christ. The cost of pursuing Him requires giving up all of oneself as Christ gave up all for us. According to Matthew 24:7–14, some will be persecuted and put to death for sharing the gospel. There will be false prophets who will deceive many people, and because of wickedness, the love of most will grow cold toward God. At one time they asked God to be with them, then they grew weary and gave in to the wickedness (*the worldly desires*) that surrounded them. Beware of the worldly desires that pull you away from God.

There will be, however, an army that stands firm to the end. God's church will prevail, and the gates of hell will not overcome the church of God. All the signs of the present age are pointing to the return of Jesus Christ. The hour is drawing near. John 9:4 issues this warning, "As long as it is day, we must do the work of him who sent me. Night is coming, when no man can work." God is going to pour out His Spirit upon the face of the earth and use every means possible to awaken the world to Christ Jesus to bring His people back to Him. God is the same yesterday, today, and forever! His power to deliver, heal, set demon-possessed people free, raise the dead, and provide food for thousands upon thousands has not diminished. He is looking for yielded vessels, individuals with a passion to follow Him. God is searching for men and women who will say, "I will die to self and believe in the works of the Master."

Be a person of passion, ignited with a desire to be like Christ. He tells us, "Believe me when I say that I am in the Father and the Father is in me; or at least believe on the evidence of the miracles themselves. I tell you the truth, anyone who has faith in me will do what I have been doing. He will do even greater things than these because I am going to the Father. And I will do whatever you ask in my name, so that the Son may bring glory to the Father. You may ask me for anything in my name, and I will do it" (John 14:11–14). This is so awesome, so deep, and full of His love we can only see a glimpse of His divine glory.

Faith is a misunderstood word today. What it really means is a total alliance, a union of marriage to our Father God. So when we see the word *faith*, we should see total alliance, total loyalty only to God. Faith is not a mental ascension saying, "I believe in God." This does not constitute faith. Rather, it is a holy vow, a covenant made with the Father, with a life completely committed to Him alone. Then when Jesus said, "I tell you the truth, anyone who has *faith in me* will do what I have been doing," He was referring to the covenant union made to Him, a total alliance, loyalty to God.

From pursuing Christ and the desire to know Him more comes a source of unspeakable joy that bubbles deep within you. God then becomes your all in all. The most blessed passionate times believers can experience are while constantly pursuing, with reverent admiration, God. There is such a surpassing greatness from knowing Him that no words can adequately express it. The apostle Paul said, "I count everything a loss compared to the surpassing greatness of knowing Christ Jesus my Lord" (Phil. 3:8). This involves knowing Him intimately, deeply, being an imitator of His divine nature. Not just hearing about Him and repeating some things He did, but establishing a real relationship with Him. John 17:3 says, "Now this is eternal life: that they may know you, the only true God, and Jesus Christ, whom you have sent."

Never ceasing, we are sustained by Christ's love.
Never ceasing, we are given life from above.
Seeking the Father, we cry thy will be done.

Crucifying self, God's glory is made known.
Yielded, His glory shines through.
Surrendered, we sing Holy, Holy, Holy.

—AUTHOR

*Jesus, Jesus, O let me see that I must die to self so that oth-
ers may live and know You. You have called me to live a
life of absolute dependence upon You, Lord. Jesus, move
upon my heart and reveal by Your Spirit what I need
to remove from my life so I can be cleansed and pursue
that life of abiding in You. Lord, let me depend upon You
every moment of the day and yield myself to You. Lord
God, give me a passion that burns within me to know
You intimately. Jesus, reveal to me, Your bride, the stains
and the condition of my garment. Jesus, may I as part of
the church arise this very hour and cry out to You for a
true revelation of the condition of my heart. Let me be
changed every moment from glory to glory. Lord, let it
be my prayer that the words of my mouth and the medi-
tation of my heart be pleasing in Your sight. I desire to
please You, my Lord. Amen.*

Chapter 7

PERSEVERANCE HAS A PRICE

THERE IS A price to pay for perseverance. Are you willing to pay the price?

Examine your life to see where you stand with Christ. To better understand the word *persevere,* it means determined to continue firmly in an action in spite of obstacles or objections, to endure, having a fixed purpose. Perseverance means to stand firmly regardless of the situation or problem, to endure, having your entire being fixed on the purpose to which you were called. First Corinthians 15:31 says, "I die every day [*over and over again during the day*]—I mean that, brothers—just as surely as I glory over you in Christ Jesus our Lord." Paul was saying that through the cross of Jesus Christ, he was crucified (*dead to self*) daily to all the desires of this world and had denied self. This was specifically mentioned so we would embrace the same way of living as Paul embraced and as Christ did before him.

Set aside daily devotion time with God to study His Word, reflect upon Him, worship Him, and earnestly pray. The Lord will reveal His will and His desire for you when you earnestly seek Him. Spend time in reflection with Him as you carefully examine your heart and attitudes each day.

Here are a few things to ask yourself: "Is my heart grateful to God for His mercy and grace? Is God number one in my life? Is pursuing God my fixed purpose in life?" Ask God to reveal His holy love and awe to your heart as you persevere in your daily walk.

To love people and souls is to have a heart of compassion for others and their spiritual condition. Your prayer life should be a time of communication with your heavenly Father. We need to be steadily attentive of our spiritual life along with our physical body, checking our thoughts and heart condition daily. For the physical body of man needs to stay crucified and dead to self so that the spiritual life in Christ can rule within us. God is searching for those who will earnestly seek Him.

The prophet Jeremiah wrote, "Then you will call upon me and come and pray to me, and I will listen to you. You will seek me and find me when you seek me with all your heart" (Jer. 29:12–13). God wants all of you—every part. When we call out, He hears.

He looks upon the heart of man to see who is earnestly seeking Him. To seek God is to go in search of God and His perfect will for your life. Following the Master requires dying to yourself daily and yielding to God daily. To those who deny self, the will of God is of utmost importance. All this matters more than your own interests. Jesus told us to seek first His kingdom and His righteousness, and all things will be given to us as well. Matthew 6:33 tells us that seeking first the kingdom of God and His righteousness must be first in our lives; not seeking things first, but God first. God is asking, *"Who is willing to listen and obey My voice?"* The price—giving up all of you, for all of Him.

The Christian who thinks of his or her salvation as merely a means of being rescued from hell and redeemed from the affliction will find it almost impossible to live dead to self and alive unto God. The life of obedience is not in his thinking, and surrendering all is more than he had planned. To understand what a Christian is called to be and live like is simple—be like Jesus Christ. The Christian is called to deny self and follow Christ, being an imitator of Him. Study the life of Christ—the only man without sin, yielded to the Father totally, full of love and all the fruit of the Spirit. Christ our example pleased not Himself, but lived only to do the will of the Father. Then He commanded us to deny ourselves and follow Him.

Christ came so that we could be united with Him. His plan is that we abide or unite with Him. As Christians, we are reflectors of Christ, imitators of Him to show the world who Christ is. Take a moment as you read the next passage and insert your name in place of Solomon. First Chronicles 28:9–10 reads, "And you, my son Solomon, acknowledge the God of your father, and serve him with wholehearted devotion and with a willing mind, for the LORD searches every heart and understands every motive behind the thoughts. If you seek him, he will be found by you; but if you forsake him, he will reject you forever."

Perseverance is the call to stand firm and endure regardless of obstacles or trials. Serve God with wholehearted devotion. To be pure in heart is to do the will of God, which is God's way, not your way or somebody else's way. Through the power of the Holy Spirit, we can remain steadfast in our commitment to do God's will His way. When Jesus walked upon the earth, He walked with an undivided heart doing only the will of the Father who sent Him. Jesus was tempted by the devil to prove that He was the Son of God by asserting His own power. The devil tempted Jesus to do the work of God in His own way instead of the way God had planned. Jesus was wise to the enemy's plan and stood firm, persevering regardless of the situation to fulfill God's perfect plan for His life.

The enemy's strategy is to get you to exalt self above God, by seeing yourself as first, not God and His kingdom. In Luke 4:13 we read about the temptation by the devil that Jesus withstood. "When the devil had finished all this tempting, he left him until an opportune time." The devil never leaves for very long. He waits for his opportunities when we are in a weakened state. Have you heard it said that the devil has a plan for everything?

We so often say we believe that God is everywhere and present at all times. Yet we live our lives as if He is not present at all when He sees our sinful life styles at all times. So it is extremely important that we stay crucified, pray daily, united in our hearts with God, and seek God's will on a daily basis. Without purity of heart, the power of God in us is severely limited. Purity of heart and the power of God go hand in hand. Willing heart and perseverance to God's divine will is what is necessary to walk in this arena. The Lord searches and knows every heart and the motives within.

Ask yourself how pure the thoughts and motives of your heart are? Could you truly answer that you love the Lord your God with all your heart, soul, and mind? Can you say that your heart is devoted to the Lord? God's greatest commandment is found in Matthew 22:37–40. Jesus replied: "'Love the Lord your God with all your heart and with all your soul and with all your mind.' This is the first and greatest commandment. And the second is like it: 'Love your neighbor as yourself.' All the Law and the Prophets hang on these two commandments.'" God walks among His people, looking upon the heart of every man. He is in search of the person who is willing to die to self. God wants to purify your heart with His consuming fire burning away all impurities. The question is, are you willing?

God can only work on a willing, yielded individual. The process of purifying can be painful to the flesh, but it brings deep joy to your soul and spirit as the process deepens. Cry out to God now as you surrender to Him, to create within you a clean purified heart; to renew a right attitude and spirit within you, fulfilling your heart's desire. For without a clean purified heart and a humble spirit, God cannot flow through you in the dimension He so desires. The power of God will fall on purified hearts willing to do God's will.

First John 4:16–17 says, "God is love. Whoever lives in love lives in God, and God in him....because in this world we are like him." Hear Jesus' words in John 17:14, 16–19, "I have given them your word and the world has hated them, for they are not of the world anymore than I am of the world.... They are not of the world, even as I am not of it. Sanctify them by the truth; your word is truth. As you sent me into the world, I have sent them into the world. For them I sanctify myself, that they too may be truly sanctified." We are called to be like Him. We are not to be of the world, but to live here as Christ lived. We are called to separate ourselves from the entrapments of the world and to show forth Christ's love shining through us to the world around us. When we live in the love of God, we are then like Him.

The life of the world is rooted in pleasing self, whereas the life of living and abiding in Christ is a union of love, where one is dead to exalting self and lives to please God our Father. Jesus sanctified Himself by setting Himself apart to only do the will of God, dying on the cross, not only to save us, but also to show us the life of consecration requires setting ourselves apart for service to the Father. Many have asked *"How do I persevere or remain in that crucified life?"* Do as Jesus did. He is our living example. Jesus lived in total alliance to God, vowing His life to total obedience to God's voice. He stayed loyally committed to only saying and doing what the Father said. Jesus has always had a holy union with the Father. Self was never an issue with Christ. Christ knew the crucified life before He ever died on the cross for us. Choose to be yielded to the Father as Christ was. Jesus humbled Himself unto death and opened the way to which we are called to follow. The fruit of death to our will is humility.

Submitting to God is the key to being humble in spirit. Consider James 4:6–10: "God opposes the proud but gives grace to the humble. Submit yourselves, then, to God. Resist the devil, and he will flee from you. Come near to God and he will come near to you. Wash your hands, you sinners, and purify your hearts, you double-minded. Grieve, mourn and wail. Change your laughter to mourning and your joy to gloom. Humble yourselves before the Lord, and he will lift you up." Humble means meek, unpretentious, not arrogant or exalting self, to be submissive. Once again humble is mentioned as a state of submission and not exalting self. Humility is giving up self on the altar of sacrifice, taking the position of nothingness before God. To the soul that maintains the pursuit of Jesus, humbling oneself and counting oneself as nothing but a yielded vessel, that is the soul crucified with Christ. The emptier the vessel placed before God, the fuller the inflow of Gods divine waters of pure life.

> Unfathomable Sea
> All life is out of Thee,
> And Thy life is Thy blissful Unity.
> —FREDERICK W. FABER

As we read Luke 4:32, 36 think of how Christ surrendered all. Verse 32 says, "They were amazed at his teaching, because his message had authority." Verse 36 says, "All the people were amazed and said to each other, 'What is this teaching? With authority and power he gives orders to evil spirits and they come out!'" The words Christ spoke were the words of the Father.

Jesus surrendered all of Himself to the will of the Father. God calls for His people to surrender all of themselves to Him each day. The cost is high, and it takes perseverance to walk a yielded life. If we die to ourselves, we live with Christ. If we endure hardships, persecutions, and trials, we will reign with

Christ. Consider the other side of this story. If you disown Christ, He will disown you. Remember, God is a jealous God ,and He will have no other gods (*idols, things, people, anything first*) before Him. Matthew tells us, "Then Jesus went with his disciples to a place called Gethsemane, and he said to them, 'Sit here while I go over there and pray.' He took Peter and the two sons of Zebedee along with him, and he began to be sorrowful and troubled. Then he said to them, 'My soul is overwhelmed with sorrow to the point of death. Stay here and keep watch with me.' [*watch and pray with me.*] Going a little farther, he fell with his face to the ground and prayed, 'My Father, if it possible, may this cup be taken from me. Yet not as I will, but as you will'" (Matt. 26:36–39). This passage is loaded with riches from God, but we want to zero in on His will. Jesus said, "Not My will, but yours, My Father." How often do we say, "*Only your will God. I will not be concerned with what man thinks, feels, or wants.*" This is the place where dead men walk. They are not concerned about their will or other people's will, only God's will. It takes a persevering spirit to do the will of God.

Will you pray with me?

> *O Lord and Savior, I can only be an imitator of You when I am one with You. I can only reflect You and Your divine character as I walk with You, abiding in You. Lord God, I surrender my life to You completely. Let me be entirely given up to You. Lord, may I be so united with You that I may live as not of this world, but in the world solely for reflecting Christ's perfect love to the world. Let Your Holy Spirit make known to me the work in the world You have planned for me to do as I yield myself totally to You. God, ignite within my heart a holy desire to pursue only You. It is my deepest desire that all the cares and things of this world fall behind me, and in their place burn a holy, con-suming fire for You and Your perfect will in my life. Lord, You called me to follow You and to bear Your image to those around me, so daily I die to self as I seek to be led*

by You moment by moment. Let this begin now, and may it grow deeper each and every day as I begin to become a man (or woman) of ignited faith. Thank You for hearing my prayer. Amen!

Chapter 8

BELIEF VS. OBEDIENCE

THERE IS NO place or position you can obtain by good works that will give you a position in the kingdom of God. It does not matter how often you attend church, read the Bible, or say a prayer. If you are in rebellion, your heart is not right. You resist the prompting of the Holy Spirit and reject Christ. You are a rebel against God. Rebellious Christians reject obedience to the Master. There are those who confess with the mouth but not from the depths of their heart. They go to church and are loyal to the principle of what their religion has taught them. They have a casual acquaintance with God at certain times, and call upon this person about which they have been informed. This form of casual acquaintanceship establishes no intimate relationship as a son or daughter with the heavenly Father. God's children have a deep love for the Father and respond to His love with a heart of faithfulness to Him. His children maintain a total loyalty to God. They are united with Him in a deep commitment.

Walking with Christ involves allowing Him to constantly change us. Having His will and way in us always takes us onward with Him. We need a right heart and a deep yearning from our depths to obey His voice and do His will. Ask yourself, *"Do I believe in God and do His commands?"* Christianity is devoted obedience to God, the voluntary submission of the soul, which means submitting your will to His divine will. It is a humbling of oneself. Many say they believe yet there is evidence in their lives they do not believe with their heart. For it is not with the mouth that one believes, or even the mind—it must come from the heart. As the writer of Hebrews warns, "Today, if you hear his voice, do not harden your hearts as you did in the rebellion, during the time of testing in the desert, where your fathers tested and tried me and for forty years saw what I did. That is why I was angry with that generation, and I said, 'Their hearts are always going astray, and they have not known my ways.' So I declared on oath in my anger, 'They shall never enter my rest.' See to it, brothers, that none of you has a sinful, unbelieving heart that turns away from the living God" (Heb. 3:7–12).

Many times the children of Israel grumbled and complained, saying it would have been much better to stay in Egyptian bondage. The same problem exists today. Many times we say it would have been better for us elsewhere. Every time a new trial or hardship comes up, the complaining starts. Just like the children of Israel, many still desire only the benefits, please, no lessons or hardships. One cannot learn from benefits alone; lessons are learned in trials and tribulations. It is in trials and tribulations our character is developed or deepened to be more like Christ—if we stay submitted to God.

James 1:2–4 tells us, "Consider it pure joy, my brothers, whenever you face trials of many kinds, because you know that the testing of your faith [*alliance and loyalty*] develops perseverance. Perseverance must finish its work so that you may be mature and complete, not lacking anything." Faith is an alliance and loyalty to God that develops your perseverance. Perseverance requires endurance, having a fixed purpose— determined to continue firmly in action despite obstacles or objections. Enduring regardless of obstacles and objections will take us into being mature, complete, and like Christ. Then one lacks nothing. Remember the words of 2 Corinthians 4:16–18, "Therefore do not lose heart. Though outwardly we are wasting away, yet inwardly we are being renewed day by day. For our light and momentary troubles are achieving for us an eternal glory that far outweighs them all. So we fix our eyes not on what is seen but on what is unseen. For what is seen is temporary, but what is unseen is eternal."

To a man in pursuit of God, even in times of trials the bitter things of life can turn to sweetness. We learn how to count all things joy, even our trials and light tribulations. These situations that arise develop our character and make us sweeter, just like Christ. He brought a sweet aroma of love to the world. This love is a mighty river that makes barren life blossom like a rose. There is no barren, dry life in the soul surrendered to the Master. When we abide in Him and He in us, everything is sweeter. For the soul that no longer seeks its own abides in the mighty river of life and bears the sweet fragrance of Christ's love.

From Jesus' parable of the sower, what kind of soil best describes us? As the farmer was sowing seed upon the ground, some fell along the path and was trampled under foot. Then the birds of the air ate the seed. Other seed fell on the rock, and when it started to come up, the tender young plant withered due to lack of water. Then some fell among the thorns, and grew up among the thorns, which choked out the seed. Finally, some seed fell on the good rich soil and yielded a crop a hundred times more than what was sown. In Luke 8:11–15 Jesus says, "This is the meaning of the parable: The seed is the word of God. Those along the path are the ones who hear, and then the devil comes and takes away the word from their hearts, so that they may not believe and be saved. [*They once heard the Word and received it but gave in to the devil's tactics.*] Those on the rock are the ones who receive the Word with joy when they hear it, but they have no root. [*These are those who are not able to endure in the trials and tribulations of life.*] They believe for a while, but in the time of testing they fall away. The seed that fell among thorns stands for those who hear, but as they go on their way they are choked by life's worries, riches and pleasures, and they do not mature. [*Those whose self is their God, and because pleasure is their desire, they are choked to death by pleasing self.*] But the seed on good soil stands for those with a noble [*godly character distinguished by godly deeds*] and good heart [*whole personality of Christ or the moral and emotional part of Christ*], who hear the word, retain it, and by persevering [*enduring all]* produce a crop [*a mature harvest*]."

Remember, the seed represents God's living Word. The devil uses several devices and avenues to steal that word from your heart and life. The devil is cunning, a great deceiver, treacherous. Do not underestimate his ability to deceive you! Do not forget the devil has had over 6,000 years of practicing deception! Satan will use times of testing, trials, tribulations, cares of the world, pleasures of the world, riches, other loved ones, individuals, your work, and many other ways to turn your heart and life from being fully committed to the Lord. Listen to the truth on pride's fall. If Satan cannot prevent you from stepping closer to God and keep you at the bottom of the staircase, he will help you climb the staircase to self-fulfillment and great success. As you exalt your name, he will help push you right over the top and oh, what a fall! Remember that there are no superstars in heaven except God. Stay humble—count yourself as nothing, but one totally yielded to God. Jesus, our living example, made Himself nothing. Jesus took on the nature of a servant and humbled Himself, submitting to the will of the Father. His total obedience to death on the cross and His nature of living are how He calls us to live.

There are many in the church today who are deceived by the enemy and his lying ways. They believe good works will get them into heaven. If they confess Jesus with their mouth it is a done deal they are heaven bound. This is so far from the truth. One's heart must be totally yielded to the will of the Father and completely obedient to the Lord. Doing good can often have a self-serving motive. It brings a person to the forefront, feeding their desires to be recognized. Therefore, it feeds their flesh. When doing the works of the Lord, all glory, praise, and honor go to the Father, not the vessel. When others exalt men continually, it is difficult not to fall into this trap of pleasing men. Beware of this trap of Satan. The flesh must be crucified daily and be dead to the snares and temptations of the enemy. When we humbly come before God in utter, total submission to Him, asking to learn to live the yielded, obedient life, He will by His Spirit begin a work within us.

God will require that you deny self and give up your will and your life to Him. This is the way to learn obedience. It is making His will your heart's desire and delight. It is being guided by the Creator who has all wisdom, knowledge, authority, power, and perfect love. The life of abiding and dwelling in Christ, having that devoted personal relationship, is found in obeying. *Oh, let us cling to God in obedience.* Obedience is learned from Jesus, our example, who patiently waits each and every moment to hear what the Father has to say. Learn to walk with God and hear His voice as He instructs you from day to day, moment by moment. For a heart yielded to God the Father is a heart that is willing to obey.

In Genesis 3:4–7, we read, "The serpent said to the woman, 'For God knows that when you eat of it your eyes will be opened, and you will be like God, knowing good and evil. When the woman saw that the fruit of the tree was good for food and pleasing to the eye, and also desirable for gaining

61

wisdom, she took some and ate it. She also gave some to her husband, who was with her, and he ate it. Then the eyes of both of them were opened, and they realized they were naked; so they sewed fig leaves together and made coverings for themselves." In examining this passage closely, we see that Satan appears as the serpent spewing his words of poison into the ears of Eve, "When you eat, your eyes will be opened, and you will be like God, exalting yourself above God or equal." (See Genesis 3:5.) This sounds quite appealing! This is the same poison Satan uses today, trying to get man to believe he can be equal to or above God, exalting himself. Remember, what sounds appealing is not always right. Only God's way is right. Satan went on to say that Eve would know good and evil and therefore be just like God. This is Satan's way of getting someone to exalt themselves above God.

This "being like God and knowing good and evil" was tempting even though God commanded Adam and Eve, "Do not eat of the tree in the midst of the garden." (See Genesis 2:9–17.) When God speaks, we need to listen to Him and Him only. He is first. Ever since Satan tried to exalt himself above God and failed, the evil one has never quit trying to get men to exalt themselves.

Eve looked and saw the fruit was good. She came to the conclusion, "This looks good, sounds good, and should benefit me." The food was good, pleasing to the eye, and desirable for gaining wisdom, so she took and ate of it. Then she gave some to her husband to eat, and he ate it willingly. Then both of their eyes were opened to the dreadful sin they committed. Now sin was exposed in their lives, and God took second place to them for they were self-pleasing, exalting self first.

In an attempt to cover up the now exposed sin, they covered themselves in the natural and in the spiritual. For when God came to see them, they hid from the Lord because they knew they had disobeyed Him. Many have attempted to cover their sins, but God sees all and knows all. Most people in the church do not fall for the obvious evils at first. It is the little things that ensnare them, such as believing something is good when it is not and goes against what God had planned. Obedience has a price, and it costs every part of you. There are no short cuts or other avenues when you decide to follow the voice of the Shepherd. The sheep know the voice of their Master, and they follow totally surrendered to His voice. John 10:25–30 says, "I did tell you, but you do not believe. The miracles I do in my Father's name speak for me, but you do not believe because you are not my sheep. My sheep listen to my voice; I know them, and they follow me. [*God's people follow and obey Him.*] I give them eternal life, and they shall never perish; no one can snatch them out of my hand. My Father, who has given them to me, is greater than all; no one can snatch them out of my Father's hand. I and the Father are one." An obedient believer cannot be forced to walk away from the voice of the Shepherd. Sheep know the Shepherd and stay focused on the Master's voice. The sheep are secure and feel the protection of the Shepherd as they obey Him. Spend time with God daily, and learn to listen to His voice.

According to James 2:19, "You believe that there is one God. Good! Even the demons believe that—and shudder." To confess with the mouth you believe there is one God does not get you entrance into heaven. If that were the case, then the demons and the devil himself would be in heaven. The key to heaven is giving yourself completely to God—obey His voice and follow only Him with all your heart. When we come near to God, He promises to come near to us. We need to purify our hearts, turn to God, and ask His forgiveness for our sins.

Jesus, we thank You for Your precious blood that washes away all our sins. Lord, expose any unknown sins in our lives, so that we may become as white as snow. Pour that precious blood over us, in Jesus' name.

The call of God has never changed, His Word has never changed, and neither have Jesus or the Holy Spirit. The Word declares that God is the same, yesterday, today and forever. Deuteronomy 11:1, 13, 26–28 instructs us to, "Love the LORD your God and keep his requirements, his decrees, his laws and his commands always....So if you faithfully obey the commands I am giving you today—to love the LORD your God and to serve Him with all your heart and with all your soul....See, I am setting before you today a blessing and a curse—the blessing if you obey the commands of the LORD your God that I am giving you today; the curse if you disobey the commands of the LORD your God and turn from the way that I command you today by following other gods, which you have not known." God explicitly tells us what He requires of His people, and that is obedience. To not live a surrendered life to the Father, to not walk in His ways, to harden your heart and disobey brings curses. So the simple truth of the matter is to choose for yourself whom you will serve and obey—God or another. Like Peter and the apostles in Acts 5:29, "We must obey God rather than men!" We read in 1 John 2:4–6, "The man who says, 'I know him,' but does not do what he commands is a liar, and the truth is not in him. But if anyone obeys his word, God's love is truly made complete in him. This is how we know we are in him: Whoever claims to live in him must walk as Jesus did." *To live in Christ is to be an imitator of Him, that is how we know we are abiding in Him and Him in us.* Reflecting Christ to those around us in the world is only possible when we are in Him abiding together as one.

In Matthew 19:17, the rich young man asked Jesus what good thing He could do to receive eternal life. Here is Jesus' reply: "Why do you ask me about what is good? There is only One who is good. If you want to enter life, obey the commandments." The rich man asked which ones, knowing there were many commandments to obey. Jesus named many of them. The rich man answered, "All these I have kept. What do I still lack?" (Matt. 19:20). *There were areas of his heart still he had not surrendered in obedience to God.* So the Lord told the rich man to sell all he had, then follow Him—put Christ first. The rich man went away sad because he had great wealth. Love of money was his idol. He could not put God first and obey Christ's command.

When we submit to God, those things that may have once looked impossible become possible. When we put our trust in God and choose to obey Him things change. "As obedient children, do not conform to the evil desires you had when you lived in ignorance. But just as he who called you is holy, so be holy in all you do; for it is written: 'Be holy, because I am holy'" (1 Pet. 1:14–16). Obedient children no longer conform to the evil desires of the world, but conform to be like Christ. Have you conformed to be like Christ?

Can you sincerely pray this prayer?

> *O blessed Lord and Savior, let me walk as You walked in obedience to the Father. Precious Jesus, let me have a heart like Yours in total submission to the Father. Jesus, You said that we are to follow You, and You did nothing of Your ownself. You only did what the Father instructed when He spoke to You. Christ Jesus, You are the perfect example of obedience to the Father, and I choose to follow after You. Amen.*

How great is God, yet how small am I.

I'm just a mere vessel, upon the altar of sacrifice.

O God of endless love, let the rivers of life flow through me.

As I embrace the cross and run the race that is set before me.

—AUTHOR

Chapter 9

FEAR OF THE LORD—A HOLY REVERENCE

WHOMEVER YOU FEAR is whom you serve! If you fear men or Satan, you will serve self or Satan. If it is God you fear, you will serve God. When serving self you are in reality serving Satan, for he has deceived you into putting yourself above God. The definition of fear used here refers a total reverence toward God, to hold in awe. Your alliance is to Him only—total loyalty. You are afraid of displeasing God because you respect and esteem Him. Reverence means to regard with mingled fear, respect, and affection. When we reverence the Lord, we walk in a holy fear with respect and loyalty. When we fear the Lord, there is a deep desire within our hearts to keep ourselves purified while we walk with the Lord. The fear of God will keep you from walking in the ways of the world. God said we are to cleanse ourselves from the things of the world. When we do so, He will dwell in us. The choice is ours, to fear Him and serve Him, or to disown Him.

Second Corinthians 6:16–18 states, "For we are the temple of the living God. As God has said; 'I will live with them and walk among them, and I will be their God, and they will be my people. Therefore come out from them and be separate, says the Lord. Touch no unclean thing, and I will receive you. I will be a Father to you, and you will be my sons and daughters, says the Lord Almighty.'" God calls us to separate from all manner of sin. When we obey then He receives us. Second Corinthians 7:1 says, "Since we have these promises, dear friends, let us purify ourselves from everything that contaminates body and spirit, perfecting holiness out of reverence to God." We *are to be known as the temple of the living God, when our temple is purified and completely cleansed.* God promises, "I will live with them and walk among them, and I will be their God, and they will be my people" (2 Cor. 6:16). When we desire to have God live with us and walk with us, we must obey Him.

Today there are men and women who were once used of God mightily, but who will not acknowledge their sins. If you are one of these people, come to the altar now, and confess your sins before God. King David was aware of his transgressions and that the Spirit of God might cast him aside like Saul. David knew that the Spirit of God was taken from this former king due to Saul's sinful living and his unrepentant heart. So David, a man after God's own heart, asked for mercy and to be purged of his sin. He knew he needed the blood of sacrifice and the cleansing water applied to his life.

God, who walked with Adam, Enoch, and Noah, wants to walk with His purified people. Genesis 3:8 tells us that Adam and Eve hid from the Lord as God walked in the garden calling to them. When sin is present, we hide from the Lord. Prior to Adam's sinning, he had walked with God in the garden.

Genesis 5:24 tells us, "Enoch walked with God; then he was no more because God took him away." Enoch was taken up to be with God. Genesis 6:9 describes Noah as a righteous man, blameless among the people of his time, who walked with God. Three different men are listed here as men who walked with God. In order to receive a promise from God, there is a requirement put upon man—give of oneself completely.

"Therefore come out from them and be separate, says the Lord" (2 Cor. 6:17). Do not become yoked with the world, unbelievers, and false teachers. Do not tie yourselves to them or unite with them in fellowship. A yoke is a bondage to a heavy load; in reality, this yoke comes from Satan. Yokes are sent to destroy, kill, and steal the individual and remove him from the presence of God. Touch no unclean thing, nothing that can remove you from being clean or purified as a spotless bride. No stains, spots, wrinkles, or blemishes do you want on your garment or temple (your body). Since we have the promise of God living with us and walking among us, let us purify ourselves from everything that contaminates body and spirit. God calls us to perfect holiness out of reverence for Him.

God's Word gets to the point in Luke 12:4–5. "I tell you, my friends, do not be afraid of these who kill the body and after that can do no more. But I will show you whom you should fear: Fear him who, after the killing of the body, has power to throw you into hell. Yes, I tell you, fear him." We are to stand in awe of the Lord, trusting Him and reverencing Him. God alone has all power; man has extremely limited power. Who is it that you truly fear—man or God? Whom do you serve, God or another? Fear is a wonderful thing in this context when it is standing in awe of God. God represents more than any words can express. When we behold Him, we will see that He is more than what we can express. God is worth more than all the world has to offer.

When we receive the gift of salvation, we accept the gift

from the giver, but we also give ourselves back to Him as a surrendered individual on the altar of sacrifice. We start a process of spiritual growth that will take an entire lifetime of perseverance and obedience, always pressing on toward the perfect will of God. God is always revealing new facets of Himself, a deeper understanding of His divine nature.

The apostle Paul writes in Philippians 2:5-7, 12:

> "Your attitude should be the same as that of Christ Jesus: Who, being in very nature God, did not consider equality with God something to be grasped, but made himself nothing, taking the very nature of a servant, being made in human likeness. [*Jesus Son of God—considered Himself nothing, but fully submitted to doing the will of the Father.*].... Therefore, my dear friends, as you have always obeyed—not only in my presence, but now much more in my absence—continue to work out your salvation with fear and trembling, for it is God who works in you to will and to act according to His good purpose."

Work it out means to keep working to achieve God's desired destination or completion for your life in Him. Salvation is not a gift received once and for all with no requirements. For you to work out your salvation requires an ongoing process of dying to self in complete dedication to God. Malachi 3:16–18 states, "Then those who feared the LORD talked with each other, and the LORD listened and heard. A scroll of remembrance was written in his presence concerning those who feared the LORD and honored his name. 'They will be mine,' says the LORD Almighty, 'in the day when I make up my treasured possession. I will spare them, just as in compassion a man spares his son who serves him. And you will again see the distinction between the righteous and the wicked, between those who serve God and those who do not.'" This again comes back to whomever you put first or serve as your master. The fear of the Lord is the key to the treasure, an intimate relationship

God desires with His people. To be a part of God's treasure and to live with Him as His son or daughter, one needs to fear, respect, esteem, reverence, and have total loyalty to God. Choose to serve God. Turn away from all manner of wickedness. Embrace the cross of Christ as you deny self and follow after Him. Decide to be a part of those who fear the Lord and pursue Him.

Solomon pursued wisdom and had great wealth, but he also had periods of torment. He realized man pursues one thing and then another as if one could somehow master this world or be a god over the world. Humans are limited, yet man acts as if he is in control of his world and can control his own destiny and eternity. This is meaningless, for what matters is a heart that is committed in its relationship to God. Isaiah 2:22 says, "Stop trusting in man, who has but a breath in his nostrils. Of what account is he?" *Man is nothing to even put your trust or loyalty in.*

Solomon came to the revelation knowledge that apart from God, all is less important in life except fearing God and keeping His commandments. He writes in Ecclesiastes 12:13–14, "Now all has been heard; here is the conclusion of the matter: Fear God and keep his commandments, for this is the whole [duty] of man. For God will bring every deed into judgment, including every hidden thing, whether it is good or evil." Remember that God sees all and knows all, and nothing is hidden from Him. The duty of man is to fear God and obey His commandments. Can you answer yes to this question: "Are you doing your duty?"

Psalm 112:1 and 111:9–10 read, "Blessed is the man who fears the LORD, who finds great delight in His commands. He provided redemption for his people; he ordained his covenant forever—holy and awesome is his name. The fear of the LORD is the beginning of wisdom; all who follow his precepts have good understanding." When Scripture refers to "holy is his name," it means perfectly perfect is the Lord. The word *holy* means to be

71

perfect (when referring to God), sacred, and spiritually pure. God has not changed; His Word is still the same. He is still holy and perfectly perfect. God wants us to conduct ourselves in the fear of the Lord. Holy and surrendered is still the call, and fearing the Lord is a part of surrendering yourself to Him. Delightful fellowship is found in fearing God.

In the tenth chapter of Leviticus we read about the deaths of Nadab and Abihu. These were the sons of Aaron who took and offered unauthorized fire before the Lord, contrary to the Lord's command. They did not fear or reverence the commands of God. They disobeyed God, and it cost them their lives. The Lord had fire come out from His presence and consumed them both. Moses then told Aaron, "This is what the Lord spoke of when he said: 'Among those who approach me I will show myself Holy; in the sight of all the people I will be honored.'" Aaron remained silent. Then the bodies of Nadab and Abihu were carried outside the camp. Aaron and His other two sons were instructed not to become unkempt or to rent their clothes, for if they did they would die also. They were also instructed not to leave the tent of meeting, or they would die because the anointing oil was upon them. So they did as they were instructed.

We see that Nadab and Abihu offered unauthorized fire before the Lord, contrary to His command. They decided they would disobey God and do as they pleased. Then the Lord came out with fire from His presence and consumed them both. Aaron and his other two sons decided that day they were going to do whatever the Lord said to them through Moses. We need to listen to the voice of the Lord and obey Him.

Acts 4:32–36 relates how the believers shared their possessions—*they are all one in heart and mind* (unified). From time to time, those who owned land or houses sold them and brought the money from the sale to the apostles. Joseph, a Levite whom the apostles called Barnabas, sold his property and brought his money to the apostles. Notice here they were all one in heart and mind, sharing and binding themselves together in unity. Then, in Acts 5, we read of Ananias and his wife, Sapphira, who also sold their property. Both of them agreed to keep back a part of the money for themselves. This was not the problem; it was their money to do with as they wished. But the spirit of lying and deception entered, and Ananias tried to deceive the Holy Spirit. He and Sapphira had planned to lie and deceive not man, but God. As soon as Ananias lied to the Holy Spirit, he fell down dead. Great fear seized all that heard what happened. This was the holy fear of the Lord that seized their hearts. Then the young men carried Ananias's body out and buried him. About three hours later, Sapphira comes, not aware of what happened to her husband. Peter asks her, "Tell me, is this the price you and Ananias got for the land?" (v. 8). Sapphira affirms the price, then Peter asks her, "How is it you agree to test the Spirit of the Lord?" He tells her that the men who buried her husband are at the door to carry her out also. At that moment she fell down dead. The men carried her out and buried her also.

Great fear captured the whole church, and all who heard about these events now had reverence, awe, loyalty, and respect for God.

In both of these cases, a new era was being set into motion. When we compare these passages in both instances, God's people needed to be made aware that they solely existed for God and not for themselves. They had to be reminded of who God was and reverence Him once more. The manifested presence of God was present in both of these cases, and yet contrary to God's commands, the persons involved had decided to do as they desired. Self became their God, and deception, lying, and disobedience, while in God's manifest presence, cost them their lives. God will not allow people to mock Him or His Holy Spirit. This is set as a warning to the church to purify herself and set the house of God in His divine order. The bride that God is coming for must be white as snow, without sin, spots, wrinkles, or blemishes. God's Word is unchangeable.

Psalm 25:12–14 says, "Who, then, is the man that fears the LORD? He will instruct him in the way chosen for him. He will spend his days in prosperity, and his descendants will inherit the land. The LORD confides in those who fear him; he makes his covenant known to them." Deuteronomy 5:29 tells us, "Oh, that their hearts would be inclined to fear me and keep all my commands always, so that it might go well with them and their children forever!" To be inclined to fear God and keep all His commands means then all will go well for you. Second Corinthians 5:11 states, "Since, then, we know what it is to fear the LORD, we try to persuade men." Whom you fear is whom you serve. Whom do you hold in reverence and awe? Do you fear displeasing God or another? Is it your prayer to fear God all the days of your life and to serve Him? Have you tried to persuade men to fear and serve God? The choice is yours.

Chapter 10

COMMITTED OR COMPROMISING?

WHAT WOULD YOUR answer be to the question, "Are you devoted to the Lord?" I am referring to the type of devotion where your desire is to obey only Him and serve no other. You want all of Him and none of self. It is not 99 percent. It is a 100 percent giving of yourself to Him and making Him Lord over your life. Being committed totally to the Lord requires a surrendered life of commitment without compromising.

Hear the words of the Lord in Luke 6:46–47. "Why do you call me, 'Lord, Lord,' and do not do what I say?' I will show you what he is like who comes to me and hears my words and puts them into practice." Let's examine the meaning of this verse. If you call Him Lord and Savior, you are saying, "He is ruler over me and has all authority over me." Be careful, for God is saying, "Do not call me Lord, when in reality I am not your Lord. I am not the One you regard as ruler with authority over you, for you are not surrendered to Me." Are you surrendered?

Will you continue to go on living your own life, taking control of your own situations and plans? If so, be aware that deception can block the heart and obstruct truth from prevailing. The more a person hardens his heart or refuses to obey the prompting of the Holy Spirit, the more obstructed the heart becomes. In Matthew 7:21 Jesus says, "Not everyone who says to me, 'Lord, Lord' will enter the kingdom of heaven, but only he who does the will of my Father, who is in heaven." In this passage, Jesus makes it rather clear that only the committed ones who do God's will enter heaven. Living in obedience, commitment without compromise, is the way to heaven. For when you are dead to self, obedience and commitment are not a problem.

The call for us to persevere in Jude 17–20 says. "But, dear friends, remember what the apostles of our Lord Jesus Christ foretold [*prophesied*]. They said to you, 'In the last times there will be scoffers [*mockers*] who will follow their own ungodly desires.' These are the men who divide you, who follow mere natural instincts [*selfishness*] and do not have the Spirit [*of God*]. But you, dear friends, build yourselves up in your most holy faith and pray in the Holy Spirit." The days in which we live were predicted in the Bible. Basically two groups of people are mentioned—the committed who walk with God, and the compromising who serve self. To be committed you build yourself up in faith and prayer. The committed heart is not full of pride, but rather broken and submitted.

Listening and doing are found in James 1:19–25.

> My dear brothers, take note [*apply it to your life*] of this: Everyone should be quick to listen, slow to speak and slow to become angry, for man's anger does not bring about the righteous [*godly*] life that God desires. Therefore, get rid of all moral filth and the evil that is so preva-

lent and humbly accept the word planted in you, which can save you. Do not merely listen to the word, and so deceive yourselves. Do what it says. Anyone who listens to the word but does not do what it says is like a man who looks at his face in a mirror, and after looking at himself, goes away and immediately forgets what he looks like. But the man who looks intently into the perfect law...not forgetting what he has heard, but doing it—he will be blessed in what he does."

God corrects those who merely listen to the Word but do not do what the Word says. Living every day with the Word hidden in your heart will cause a transformation within you. Let the Word of God live in you and dwell in you in all its fullness. Live the committed life without compromising, for in it is joy and delight. We should do what the writer of the Psalm teaches: "I have hidden your word in my heart that I might not sin against you...I meditate on your precepts and consider your ways. I delight in your decrees; I will not neglect your word" (Ps. 119:11, 15–16). I have committed Your Word to my heart and reflect Your ways. I will not compromise or neglect Your Word, for it is delight and joy to my soul. Examine the life of a dead man walking, and you will find a person living the committed life to Christ. A dead man walking abides in the cross of Christ continually as he offers himself upon the altar of living sacrifice.

Psalm 50:4–6, 16–17, 21 state, "He summons the heavens above, and the earth, that he may judge his people: 'Gather to me my consecrated [*dedicated*] ones, who made a covenant [*commitment*] with me by sacrifice [*surrendering self*].' And the heavens proclaim his righteousness, for God himself is judge....But to the wicked, God says: 'What right have you to recite my laws or take my covenant on your lips? You hate my instruction and cast my words behind you.' ...These things you have done and I have kept silent; you thought I was altogether like you. But I will rebuke you and accuse you to your face." Nothing is hidden from the Lord Almighty. The most important decision in all the world is whom you shall serve! Are you committed to God, or do you compromise?

Jesus teaches in Matthew 6:24, "No one can serve two masters. Either he will hate the one and love the other, or he will be devoted [*committed*] to the one and despise the other." Since you cannot serve two masters, you must decide today who your master is. Regardless of your decision, know this— God is everywhere. The life of compromising has its price. The life of commitment is eternal life with Christ.

Psalm 139:1–8 says, "O Lord, you have searched me and you know me. You know when I sit and when I rise; you perceive my thoughts from afar. You discern my going out and my lying down; you are familiar with all my ways. Before a word is on my tongue you know it completely, O Lord. You hem me in— behind and before; you have laid your hand upon me. Such knowledge is too wonderful for me, too lofty for me to attain. Where can I go from your Spirit? Where can I flee from your presence? If I go up to the heavens, you are there; if I make my bed in the depths, you are there [*no one shall escape God*]." God, the creator of all things, sees you, hears you, watches you, and knows your thoughts and words before they ever proceed from your mouth. God is everywhere you go. Watch and pray and stay committed to the Lord, for the day is approaching when He shall return. Be ready. Allow the power of the blood to flow freely through you as it cleanses and sanctifies. The power of the blood is able to keep you daily in God's presence by its divine life-giving power. Choose to bear the cross daily. For the Lord is coming back for His people who are washed in the blood with garments as white linen.

God knows you completely and asks for your commitment to Him. We read the cost of being a disciple in Luke 14:26–27. "If anyone comes to me and does not hate his father and mother, his wife and children, his brothers and sisters—yes, even his own life—he cannot be my disciple. And anyone who does not carry [*attain*] his cross [*death to self*] and follow me cannot be my disciple." This passage is saying that you must love Jesus more than any immediate family or even yourself. It comes back to who is first place in your life, Jesus or someone else. You can only commit to one master. This is the place where dead men walk who follow Christ. Let's look at Judas and Peter in Matthew 26:14–16. "Then one of the twelve—the one called Judas Iscariot—went to the chief priests and asked, 'What are you willing to give me if I hand him over to you?' [*Selfish desire took over.*] So they counted out for him thirty silver coins. From then on Judas watched for an opportunity to hand him over." Notice he asked, "What are you willing to give me?" He wanted to benefit from this transaction. Greed was present. He loved money and his own self more than he loved Jesus. Judas chose who was going to be his master, and he wanted immediate benefits for himself. He was not committed to Christ.

Speaking to Peter, Jesus said, "'I tell you the truth...this very night, before the rooster crows, you will disown [*renounce*] me three times.' But Peter declared, 'Even if I have to die with you, I will never disown [*renounce*] you.' And all the other disciples said the same" (Matt. 26:34–35). When Jesus was arrested, all the disciples deserted Him and fled. The same disciples who walked with Him were nowhere in sight. Peter said to Jesus, "If I have to die with you, I will never disown [renounce] you Lord." The disciples lacked commitment at that time. However, as we continue to read, we see a transformation in them. They become committed to denying self and following Christ, no matter the cost.

Matthew 26:69–75 tells us, "Now Peter was sitting out in the courtyard, and a servant girl came to him. 'You also were with Jesus of Galilee,' she said. But he denied it before them all. 'I do not know what you are talking about,' he said. Then he went out to the gateway, where another girl saw him and said to the people there, 'This fellow was with Jesus of Nazareth.' He denied it again, with an oath: 'I don't know the man!' After a little while, those standing there went up to Peter and said, 'Surely you are one of them, for your accent gives you away.' Then he began to call down curses on himself and he swore to them, 'I do not know the man!' Immediately a rooster crowed. Then Peter remembered the word Jesus had spoken: 'Before the rooster crows, you will disown [*renounce*] me three times.' And he went outside and wept bitterly."

Once again we see the "self" issue. Peter knew it would not benefit him to acknowledge being one of the twelve. He was acting in self-preservation and denied Jesus. Walking in the committed life to Christ has a price; we must die to self and give God control of our life. Committed to Christ is the call, compromising is missing the mark. Peter, however, was quick to repent, for he went outside and wept bitterly over his sin. Judas noticed his own sin, but remorse was not enough. He would not turn from his selfishness. Judas went further into sin by not repenting, and he hanged himself. Peter stayed committed once he learned the crucified life in Christ. Abiding in Christ daily is the call of the believer. The choice is yours to make, committed to Christ or living the compromised life of self. The question is, where, or to whom, are your heart and life committed?

Valley of Broken Pieces

My spirit was high, my life a song,
My heart was proud, my will was strong.
Then one day came the voice of Jesus,
And I saw a Valley of Broken Pieces.

As an eagle I soared, untouched and high.
I'd rather have stayed up there in the sky.
But quietly called the voice of Jesus:
"Come to the Valley of Broken Pieces."

Down I swooped, and was filled with awe,
At the beautiful, fearful things I saw!
Yet comes the comforting words of Jesus:
"I am here in the Valley of Broken Pieces."

"Brokenness is the best gift I give.
I ask you to die, that others may live.
It is your choice," challenged the voice of
Jesus, "Rest in the Valley of Broken Pieces."

"Lo, I am with you, have no fear,
I'll teach you to love, and bring others cheer.
Forgiveness is yours," assured my Jesus,
"Only in the Valley of Broken Pieces."

I went to the valley, and saw the "I."
I saw the pride which had to die.
I found new freedom—release—in Jesus;
And wholeness now, instead of pieces!

Once I thought "I" could do it all.
Now at my Savior's feet I fall.
I am just a vessel, to be filled with Jesus,
Which He created from broken pieces.

Yes, I was broken so I might be healed.
When self was strong, Christ was concealed.
Now through me shines the light of Jesus.
Oh, blessed Valley of Broken Pieces!
—CAROL MICKELSON

Chapter 11

WHERE IS YOUR HEART?

GOD CALLS BY His Spirit, "Do you truly want to be broken? Is death to self your aim in life? Is Christ the light that you desire to shine through you to others?" Ponder these questions in your heart. We ask the Lord to draw near, and we ask for more of Him, but is it our heart's desire? The Lord hears our cries, and as He draws near, so often we then flee. God wants a humbled *(submissive)* and contrite *(repentant)* heart in which He can work. Is it possible to give your heart to God, yet try to cling to your selfish desires?

In the Valley of Broken Pieces, you will find the altar where you embrace the crucified life. It is a valley of dependence upon God, where you are broken for Him so you may be used for His glory and honor. This poem has been my favorite for many years. Yet for a long time, I had refused to submit to this place of brokenness, for fear of not being in control. I awakened one day to the fact that when self reigned, Christ was concealed. Then through deep searching and crying out to God, I requested He reveal the true condition of my heart and give me a heart like Jesus. I had come to the valley of decision and chose to lay my life on the altar of total sacrifice, doing the will of God my Father. The words "take up your cross and follow me" spelled out my daily mission in life. I pray that the message revealed in these pages awakens you also to abiding in the crucified life.

God is a consuming fire. By purifying the hearts of people who call out to Him, God enables us to come nearer to Him and Him to us. It is our choice to surrender to Him. We must desire to turn away from our sin and not be self-consumed but submitted to God, then He will purify us with His Word. "Here I am," He says. Just turn away from your sins. I will purify you with the purifying fire of my Word." This is simply surrendering on your part. Laying your life down, turning from sin, and totally obeying His commands is your choice. Answer the call to give your entire being to Him.

When we allow God to have all of us (*our heart, mind, body, soul, and spirit*) He then can use us and transform us. In return, we transform the world and those around us. First Samuel 12:23–25 speaks of the heart, "And I will teach you the way that is good and right. But be sure to fear the LORD and serve him faithfully with all your heart; consider what great things he has done for you. Yet if you persist in doing evil, both you and your king will be swept away." Notice the command *be sure to fear* (*reverence, awe*) the Lord, serving Him faithfully with all your heart. We are not to follow after the evil things of this world; rather we are to faithfully serve God with total devotion and fear. For He will teach you the way to walk—that is His way.

In 2 Chronicles 34:31, "The king stood by the pillar and renewed the covenant in the presence of the LORD—to follow the LORD and keep his commands, regulations and decrees with all his heart and all his soul, and to obey the words of the covenant written in this book." Just as the king renewed his covenant vow to the Lord, so we can renew or rededicate our vow to Him. Renewing your vow is to have a repentant, broken, and submissive heart. Psalm 42:1–2 says, "As the deer pants for streams of water, so my soul pants for you, O God. My soul thirsts for God, for the living God. When can I go and meet with God?" When your soul searches for God, earnestly seeking Him, then you will find Him. When the heart longs for God, as one who is desperate to quench their thirst, then the heart is yearning and searching for that intimate relationship found only in Him.

Paul writes this prayer in Ephesians 3:14–21: "For this reason I kneel before the Father, from whom his whole family in heaven and on earth derives its name. I pray that out of his glorious riches he may strengthen you with power through his Spirit in your inner being, so that Christ may dwell in your hearts through faith. [*He can only dwell in you if you believe in Him with complete faith.*] And I pray that you, being rooted and established in love, may have power, together with all saints, to grasp how wide and long and high and deep is the love of Christ, and to know this love that surpasses knowledge—that you may be filled to the measure of all fullness of God. Now to him who is able to do immeasurably more than we ask or imagine, according to his power that is at work within us, to him be glory in the church and in Christ Jesus throughout all generations, for ever and ever! Amen." We are called to live a life worthy of the calling we have received, being completely humble, gentle, patient, and loving. The love of Christ will be shed abroad in a heart that is surrendered to Him. Ask God to give you the greatest gift of all, and that is His love.

Next, let's look at something God detests. Psalm 5:4–6, 9–10 states, "You are not a God who takes pleasure in evil; with you the wicked cannot dwell. The arrogant cannot stand in your presence; you hate all who do wrong. You destroy those who tell lies; bloodthirsty and deceitful men the LORD abhors.... Not a word from their mouth can be trusted; their heart is filled with destruction. Their throat is an open grave; with their tongue they speak deceit. Declare them guilty, O God! Let their intrigues [*selfishness*] be their own downfall. Banish them for their many sins, for they have rebelled against you." This is what happens to those who refuse to turn to God, who rebel against His authority and commands. Remember, rebellion is rejecting God as your Master. Do not allow your own selfishness to be your downfall. The person who says in his heart, "Forgive me, God," then turns from his sin, God hears his prayer and answers. Second Timothy 2:19 says, "Nevertheless, God's solid foundation stands firm, sealed with this inscription: 'The Lord knows those who are his,' and 'Everyone who confesses the name of the Lord must turn away from wickedness.'" The turning repentant heart will die to selfishness. Psalm 51:2, 10, 17 declare, "Wash away all my iniquity and cleanse me from my sin....Create in me a pure heart, O God, and renew a steadfast spirit within me....The sacrifices of God are a broken spirit; a broken and contrite heart, O God, you will not despise." A heart surrendered to God that no longer exalts self is a broken (*separated*), contrite (*repentant*) heart. The person who sacrifices (surrenders) their separated spirit man to God will find Him. God will not disregard or disgrace the separated repentant heart and spirit. The heart that is broken is one Jesus can shine through, because the broken heart is a crucified heart. When it is pierced with the sword of God's Word and the cross, the heart will flow with the water of life.

"Teach me your way, O LORD, and I will walk in your truth; give me an undivided heart, that I may fear your name. I will praise you, O LORD my God, with all my heart; I will glorify your name forever" (Ps. 86:11–12). The undivided, steadfast, and pure heart is the surrendered heart to God. He will teach you to walk in His ways when you submit to Him. Songs of praise arise from the undivided heart to God in love and adoration.

According to Psalm 119:1–11, "Blessed are they whose

ways are blameless, who walk according to the law of the LORD. Blessed are they who keep his statues and seek him with all their heart. They do nothing wrong; they walk in his ways. You have laid down precepts that are to be fully obeyed. Oh, that my ways were steadfast in obeying your decrees! Then I would not be put to shame when I consider all your commands. I will praise you with an upright heart as I learn your righteous laws. I will obey your decrees; do not utterly forsake me. How can a young man keep his way pure? By living according to your word. I seek you with all my heart; do not let me stray from your commands. I have hidden your word in my heart that I might not sin against you." "How can I keep my heart pure?" is answered by abiding and dwelling in God's Word. Seek God with all your heart and stay committed to Him alone, and you will stay pure. Choose to become a surrendered vessel for Christ to fill.

Proverbs 4:20–23 says, "My son, pay attention to what I say; listen closely to my words. Do not let them out of your sight, keep them within your heart; for they are life to those who find them and health to a man's whole body. Above all else, guard your heart, for it is the wellspring of life." Our duty is to keep watch over our hearts, for it is our source of life. The warning is given to us to listen to God and His Word, and never let His Word be drawn away from us. For His Word is life to our heart and being. In the valley of submission is where the heart finds the source of life.

"Make a tree good and its fruit will be good, or make a tree bad and its fruit will be bad, for a tree is recognized by its fruit. [*This is referring to people and the good or bad that flows out from them.*] You brood of vipers, how can you who are evil say anything good? For out of the overflow of the heart the mouth speaks. The good man brings good things out of the good stored up in him, and the evil man brings evil things out of the evil stored in him. But I tell you that men will have to give account on the day of judgment for every careless word they have spoken. For by your words you will be acquitted, and by your words you will be condemned" (Matt. 12:33–37). Jesus was speaking to the Pharisees, or religious leaders. He still tells us this today. Whatever is in the heart in full measure will come out through the mouth. Beware of what you store within your heart, for it will flow out of you to those around you. For we will be held accountable for what we say and do. Is Christ concealed, or is He the light reflecting through you to others? Luke 12:34 says, "For where your treasure is, there your heart will be also." If it is anger and doubt, you speak it and live it. If its faith and love, you speak it and live it. If your treasure is in Christ and He in you, then you will shine with the light of Christ.

Hebrews 4:7, 12–13 tells us, "Today, if you hear his voice, do not harden your hearts....For the word of God is living and active. Sharper than any double-edged sword, it penetrates even to dividing soul and spirit, joints and marrow; it judges the thoughts and attitudes of the heart. Nothing in all creation is hidden from God's sight. Everything is uncovered and laid bare before the eyes of him to whom we must give an account." God sees all things and knows all things. What you may think you are hiding is not really hidden from Him. God knows the innermost depths of your being, even your secret thoughts. God calls us to come to Him. He waits for us to turn from our sins, to wash ourselves with His Word, giving ourselves totally to Him. God wants to see you with a pure clean heart, living for Him. Do a checkup on your heart condition; is it set on serving God fully?

My prayer is:

> God, create within me a clean heart, and renew a right spirit within me today. Father, I want to walk in Your ways; obeying Your commands. It is my desire to do the will of the Father. Show me if I have become accustomed to some things in my life that need removing. Lord, show

me Your way and Your plans as I renounce my sins and give myself to You as a clean surrendered vessel. God, show me how to die to self more and more each day, for it is my desire to become a dead man (or woman) walking for You. Lord, I come before You with sincerity of heart. With an earnest cry from my soul, O Lord, I want You to have all of me; I surrender myself anew to You today. I desire to abide in Your presence, O Lord. Arouse within me a deeper love and holy reverence for You, so I may run the race set before me. I will praise Your Holy name, as You reveal Your ways to me. In Jesus' most precious name, Amen!

You have now requested a new condition for your heart. So listen to God's Word, and stay submitted. For the heart surrendered to Christ has found the greatest treasure.

Chapter 12

IMITATORS OF GOD (FOLLOWERS)

W E IMITATE OUR Lord by doing and saying what He commands. He calls us to follow Him, denying self and
reflecting Christ in our lives. He is our Great Com-
mander in Chief; He commands, we obey. The Lord has
supreme authority over us, if following Him is our desire. Imitators are followers. They copy the pattern or role model given
them. They are known as reproductions of an original.

As a child, did you ever try to follow your dad's footprints?
In the north, where it snows, you can see footprints on the
white landscape. When I was younger, I would look for
footprints in the snow, preferably my dad's, because of his
large footprints. I could follow those large footprints right to
the front door of the house. Now my goal has changed. I want

to follow the Lord's steps and pattern my life after His. Christ is our perfect example of an imitator of God. Jesus followed in His Father's footsteps every step of His life, as our living example. In Ephesians 5:1–2, the apostle Paul teaches, "Be imitators of God, therefore, as dearly loved children and live a life of love, just as Christ loved us and gave himself up for us as a fragrant offering and sacrifice to God." We are called to live as children of light, reflecting Christ in us and to those around us. Be imitators; act and pattern yourself after Christ. Follow after Him in His footprints left behind for you. This is done when you live your life in Christ and He in you. To be followers, believers are called to live a life of love. We cannot see God, yet we know from our living for Him that He exists. For He lives in us, and we are wholly given up to Him.

Ephesians 4:17–24 tells us, "So I tell you this, and insist on it in the Lord, that you must no longer live as the Gentiles do, in the futility of their thinking. They are darkened in their understanding and separated from the life of God because of the ignorance that is in them due to the hardening of their hearts. Having lost all sensitivity, they have given themselves over to sensuality so as to indulge in every kind of impurity, with a continual lust for more. You, however, did not come to know Christ that way. Surely you heard of him and were taught in him in accordance with the truth that is in Jesus. You were taught, with regard to your former way of life, to put off your old self, which is being corrupted by its deceitful desires; to be made new in the attitude of your minds; and to put on the new self, created to be like God in true righteousness and holiness." Since we have come to Christ and put off our old selfish nature along with its evil desires, we are called to become new in the attitude of our minds. We control our minds and thoughts. We cleanse the mind and put on the new life in Christ. The lifestyle we choose is the lifestyle we wear. God created us for the purpose to be like Him—righteous and holy followers of His divine nature. The path of obedience perfects the heart and opens us up to walk as a follower of Christ. If self is alive and reigning then being an imitator of Christ and His perfect love is impossible. First Thessalonians 1:6 says, "You become imitators of us [*Paul, Silas, and Timothy*] and of the Lord." Paul and the others understood they were to be imitators of God and His nature, and they encouraged believers to do the same. Christ made a path for the believer that we are called to follow. The disciples recognized Christ's path and example of living in God's perfect will. We learn in Philippians 3:17–18, "Join with others in following my example, brothers, and take note of those who live according to the pattern we gave you. For, as I have often told you before and now say again even with tears, many live as enemies of the cross of Christ." Paul is encouraging us to follow the examples of others before us. Notice the pattern they left for us as we live according to the pattern of the Lord. He also warns, with tears of sorrow, that many live as enemies of the cross of Christ our Lord. Christ talked daily to His Father many times over issues. Christ did the will of the Father, obeyed His every command, and loved all people. Talking to the Father is a pattern we need to follow. Imitators of His pattern abide in the cross of Christ. They deny self daily and choose the crucified life.

In Matthew 16:24–26, "Jesus said to his disciples, 'If anyone would come after me, he must deny himself and take up his cross and follow me. For whoever wants to save his life will lose it, but whoever loses his life for me will find it. What good will it be for a man if he gains the whole world, yet forfeits his soul? Or what can a man give in exchange for his soul?'" When you deny yourself, you cease to make self the center of your life and actions. *(Self dies.)* When you take up the cross, you die to self. There are those who say, "I just cannot deny my selfish life to live only for God." That individual might as well say, "I am god of my life and world." That physical life you possess has just cost you life eternal. Jesus asked, "What good is it for you to gain the entire world now and every pleasure therein, and then lose your soul?" What is of such great value that you would sell your soul for it?

Read Jesus' words again in Mark 8:34–38. "Then he called the crowd to him along with his disciples and said: 'If anyone would come after me, he must deny [*disown*] himself and take up his cross [*death to self*] and follow me [*imitate me*]. For whoever wants [*it is freedom of choice*] to save his life will lose it, but whoever loses his life for me and for the gospel will save it. What good is it for a man to gain the whole world, yet forfeit his soul? Or what can a man give in exchange for his soul? If anyone is ashamed of me and my words in this adulterous and sinful generation, the Son of Man will be ashamed of him when he comes in his Father's glory with the holy angels.'" The individual who is ashamed of Jesus and His Word—more concerned what people think about them than imitating Christ—will have no part in God's kingdom. Is this world worth your soul going to hell? The younger generation is not concerned about what people think, nor do they care. This can be used in a very powerful way. We as believers in Christ need to only be concerned about what God wants us to be—not what others think or care about. For to not get intimidated by people, but surrendered to God, one must die to self and follow after Him. Jesus was not intimidated by man but rather followed the will of His Father only. Christ displayed perfect surrender of His self to the Father as our living example. As Christ displayed total dependence upon the Father day after day, we are to do likewise.

God commands us not to grieve the Holy Spirit. Ephesians 4:30 says, "And do not grieve the Holy Spirit of God, with whom you were sealed for the day of redemption." Just as people can be grieved and turned away by our actions, so the Holy Spirit will turn away and be grieved by our conduct and actions. Let's beware of how we treat the Third Person of the Trinity, because He can be grieved by bitterness, wrathful vengeance, anger, slandering, and evil speaking. He is grieved by anything contrary to demonstrating kindness and compassion to one another in love, bearing about the fruit of the Spirit. He is part of God and sent to teach us and guide us. When we submit to God, then the Holy Spirit and God's Word can instruct us on how to be Christlike. Choose to conform to the character of Christ.

Ephesians 4:31–32 tells us to "Get rid of all bitterness, rage and anger, brawling and slander, along with every form of malice. Be kind and compassionate to one another, forgiving each other, just as in Christ God forgave you." As we have received from Christ His kindness, compassion, and forgiveness, likewise we are to be kind, compassionate, and forgiving as followers of Him. This illustrates to those around us Christ's love within us. He also tells us to get rid of sin, naming some specifically. "But among you there must not be even a hint of sexual immorality, or any kind of impurity, or of greed, because these are improper for God's holy people. Nor should there be obscenity, foolish talk or course joking, which are out of place, but rather thanksgiving. For of this you can be sure: no immoral, impure or greedy person—such a man is an idolater—has any inheritance in the kingdom of Christ and of God. Let no one deceive you with empty words, for because of such things God's wrath comes on those who are disobedient. Therefore do not be partners with them [*followers of the world*]. For you were once darkness, but now you are light in the Lord. Live as children of light (for the fruit of the light consists in all goodness, righteousness, and truth) and find out what pleases the Lord. Have nothing to do with the fruitless deeds of darkness, but rather expose them. For it is shameful even to mention what the disobedient do in secret. But everything exposed by the light becomes visible, for it is light that makes everything visible. This is why it is said: 'Wake up, O sleeper, rise from the dead, and Christ will shine on you.' Be very careful, then, how you live—not as unwise but as wise, making the most of every opportunity, because the days are evil" (Eph. 5:3–16). Paul is telling us to beware, the days are evil, so be careful in whom you follow. As believers, live for Christ every day and keep yourself dead to sin. We are not to be followers of this world's evilness and sin. For we are assured if we have idols in our life, we do not have eternal life. To live as Christ, one will reflect the fruit of the Spirit. Become a partner with the Holy Trinity and a follower of Christ. The fruit of Christ's Spirit is love, joy, peace, patience, kindness, goodness, faithfulness, gentleness, and self-control. As believers who live by the Spirit, let us keep step with the Spirit. For what reason is your existence here on earth, if not to be a follower of Christ?

In Ephesians 6:10–18 we read, "Finally, be strong in the Lord and in His mighty power. Put on the full armor of God so that you can take your stand against the devil's schemes. For our struggle is not against flesh and blood, but against the rulers, against authorities, against the powers of this dark world and against the spiritual forces of evil in the heavenly realms. Therefore put on the full armor of God, [*we dress for battle*] so that when the day of evil comes, you may be able to stand your ground, and after you have done everything, to stand [*staying firm in Christ*]. Stand firm, then, with the belt of truth buckled around your waist, with the breastplate of righteousness in place, and with your feet fitted with the readiness that comes from the gospel of peace. In addition to all this, take up the shield of faith, with which you can extinguish all the flaming arrows of the evil one. Take the helmet of salvation and the sword of the Spirit, which is the word of God. And pray in the Spirit on all occasions with all kinds of prayers and requests. With this is mind, be alert and always keep on praying for all the saints."

As soldiers in the army of God, and imitators of God, we need to be dressed for battle daily. If you noticed, it is your duty to put on these garments. Be ready at all times, daily abiding with God in prayer. Standing firm, we are called to stay alert, watch, and pray for all the saints in the body of

Christ. Prayer is often overlooked in this armor wearing and battle dressing. It does little good if we attempt to dress for battle without getting our commands from our Father. Prayer is intimate communication to the Father, and we need to hear His instructions to us daily, just as Christ hears from Him daily. One cannot battle the enemy without instructions from the Father first, so prayer is essential for the believer. When the enemy keeps you from praying, he is not concerned about you defeating him in battle. For to win against the enemy, first you must seek instructions from the Father in prayer. Christ received His instructions from the Father, so we are to receive from Him. In 1 Corinthians 4:15–16 it says, "Even though you have ten thousand guardians in Christ, you do not have many fathers, for in Christ Jesus I became your father through the gospel. Therefore I urge you to imitate me." When we imitate God, we follow after His character. As Christians we should know the character of the Father. Christ knows the Father and reflects the Father to us as our living example. God is perfect love with all the fruits of the Spirit in Him with righteousness and truth. Are we bearing the fruits of His Spirit to those around us?

God is love, and in Deuteronomy 6:4–8 it says, "Hear, O Israel: The LORD our God, the LORD is one. Love the LORD your God with all your heart and with all your soul and with all your strength. These commandments that I give you today are to be upon your hearts. Impress them to your children. Talk about them when you sit at home and when you walk along the road, when you lie down and when you get up." This kind of love requires all of one's self, living a life of commitment with God first and all else secondary. It is our duty to teach others to follow Him. When we show the love of Christ to others, we show that Christ dwells in us. Let your steps be ordered of the Lord as you follow Him. Live only and wholly to the Father, as Christ our living example displayed for us to follow. Isaiah wrote, "This is what the LORD says—your Redeemer, the Holy

One of Israel: 'I am the LORD your God, who teaches you what is best for you, who directs you in the way you should go. If only you had paid attention to my commands, your peace would have been like a river, your righteousness like the waves of the sea'" (Isa. 48:17–18). The Lord, your Redeemer, will teach you and direct you when you obey His commands. It is vitally important that we obey His commands, so He can teach us and direct us in the way we should go. By listening to God as He speaks and instructs you, then following Him, you become an imitator of His divine nature. Let the peace of God fill you as you follow Him, saying this prayer:

> *Father God, as I deny myself and relinquish all of me into Your hands. I humbly ask, Lord, that You help equip me as I follow after You. Lord, it is my desire to be like You every day of my life. I want to be a reflector of Christ's character to those around me. Lord God, direct me in the way that I should go today. Lord God, let me follow in Christ's footprints that were left behind for me to walk in. Lord, may the Holy Spirit reveal to me the steps that You have predestined for me to walk in, before the beginning of time. Amen.*

Chapter 13

ABIDING IN GOD'S PRESENCE AND MANIFESTED GLORY

ERE WORDS CANNOT nourish the soul, only God Himself can by His divine Holy Spirit. He desires to bring His people to the table to feast with Him. Tasting of His goodness through an intimate relationship with God satisfies the hunger and the longing that burns within the soul of man. God desires to ignite a fire within your soul that will burn bright and consume every inch of you.

To pursue God we must acknowledge the fact we are called to lay down all things of the world and willingly submit to His will. The very second you enter into the realm where He becomes your all in all, you then step away from the world's grand illusion. The world's enticing parade ceases to exist when you are consumed with abiding in God's presence.

In chapter two, "Godlessness or Godliness?", we looked at these choices, is it God or selfish desires, God or money, God or another individual, is God first or second? Who or what do you put above God? You may say He is first, but the choices you make day in and day out speak clearly about who is truly first. Calling out for all of God requires a dying to self, taking up the cross and following Him. His glory is revealed to dead men. If His manifested glory comes upon the church while sin abounds within His church, then some could be dying as surely as Ananias and Sapphira did.

There is a difference between His presence from the anointing and the manifested glory of God. The glory of the Lord is His divine splendor, brilliance or shed radiance (*emitting light*). Manifested glory means to make visible or clearly revealing His emitting light of shed radiance. The difference in His glory and anointing is like a drop of His oil versus a great flood outpouring of His shed radiance of light. As there are facets to God, the same is true of His presence, anointing, and levels of His manifested glory. You heard it said, "The anointing and presence of God is so heavy in here." This expression describes how we can feel His presence or anointing strongly. The word *presence* means, "feeling the nearness of God." The time is coming soon when more of God's people will say, "Oh, the glory (*shed radiance*) of God filled the place." The church has to progress further before we can enter into His manifested glory. One day we will get there, because His glory will cover the whole earth.

In the year King Uzziah died, Isaiah saw the Lord seated on the throne, high and exalted, and the train of His robe filled the temple. Isaiah saw the Lord in His shed radiance. The seraphs (angels) were calling to one another. As stated in Isaiah 6:3-4, "'Holy, holy, holy is the LORD Almighty; the whole earth is full of His glory.' At the sound of their voices the doorposts and thresholds shook and the temple was filled with smoke.'" After the angels cried out, "Holy," there was a shaking before the glory ever filled the temple. A great shaking is happening in different places across the land. This modern-day shaking is a stage coming to pass before the glory fills the temple. The shaking is the cleansing stage to remove that which is not like Him.

Doorposts are a passageway leading to the entrance, or means of approach to access the door. A threshold is defined as a point of beginning or beginning stage, the base or foundation. The entrance into His glory always begins with the shaking of all that is in you, which is not like Him. This shaking is to awaken us, so we will submit to being washed and having all spots, wrinkles and blemishes upon our garment removed. The scene he witnesses in chapter 6 causes Isaiah to declare, "Woe to me!" Woe means, "overwhelmed with sorrow or deep regret." "I am ruined [*destroyed*]! For I am a man of unclean lips, and I live among a people of unclean lips, and my eyes have seen the King, the LORD Almighty" (Isa. 6:5). Isaiah saw the King, Lord Almighty in all His glory. From his expression alone, we should see how vital it is to be clean. Read the sixth chapter of Isaiah and study it.

Ezekiel 10:4 states, "Then the glory of the LORD rose from above the cherubim [*another type of angel*] and moved to the threshold of the temple. The cloud filled the temple, and the court was full of the radiance of the glory of the LORD." Once again the threshold—the point of beginning stage—is mentioned. Ezekiel goes on to describe, "And I saw the glory of the God of Israel coming from the east. His voice was like the roar of rushing waters, and the land was radiant with His glory.... The glory of the LORD entered the temple through the gate facing east. Then the Spirit lifted me up and brought me into the inner court, and the glory of the LORD filled the temple" (Ezek. 43:2, 4–5). Ezekiel 44:4–5 says, "Then the man brought me by the way of the north gate to the front of the temple. [N*otice both of these passages have gates or entrances to them.*] I looked and saw the glory of the LORD filling the temple of the LORD, and I fell face down [*knocked down face down*]. The LORD said to me, 'Son of man, look carefully, listen closely and give attention to everything I tell you concerning all the regulations [*rules and laws*] regarding the temple of the Lord. Give attention to the entrance [*way in*] of the temple and all the exits [*ways out*] of the sanctuary.'" Ezekiel 44:23 instructs, "They are to teach my people the difference between the holy and the common and show them how to distinguish between the unclean and the clean."

The Lord said for us to look, listen, and pay attention to His rules. Give attention to the way in or the passage leading to the temple of His manifested glory. The way in is through the passage of sacrifice—the altar of total submission. At the beginning point, we are to know the difference between what is holy and common and unclean and clean. To approach God unclean when His glory is present can be very dangerous. As Isaiah cried out, "Woe to me, I am ruined." Once the coal touched Isaiah's lips, his guilt was taken away and his sin was atoned for. Isaiah cried out, "Woe to me, I am ruined," because instantly he knew how impossible it was to behold the King of Glory with any guilt of sin upon Him.

Luke 9:23–27 tells us about His glory. Jesus said, "If anyone would come after me, he must deny himself and take up his cross daily and follow me. For whoever wants to save his life will lose it, but whoever loses his life for me will save it. What good is it for a man to gain the whole world, and yet lose or forfeit his very self? If anyone is ashamed of me and my words, the Son of Man will be ashamed of him when he comes in his glory and in the glory of the Father and of the holy angels. I tell you the truth, some who are standing here will not taste death before they see the kingdom of God." If you are ashamed of God and His Son, when He comes, He will be ashamed of you and you will miss out on the glory of God. God is calling, "Keep yourself cleaned daily, and do not forsake me. Draw near to me; seek me and follow me." When He comes in His glory, will you be with those who go to be with Him? When Jesus said, "Some who are standing here will not taste death before they see the kingdom of God," God tells His people to be ready at all times for Him. Are you ready for Him?

In Luke 24, we read about two men walking and talking (on the road to Emmaus) with Jesus. Jesus had suddenly appeared walking along with them, but they are kept from recognizing Him. Jesus asks them, "What are you talking about?" They tell Jesus of a prophet who is powerful in word and deed. He was sentenced to death and died before God and all the people. The two men were discussing Jesus' crucifixion. They went on to explain how some women found His tomb empty and how the angels came and declared He was alive. Then others went to the tomb to see. It was just as the women had announced. All this time the two men are walking and talking to Jesus, never recognizing who He was. Jesus was present with the two men, but He was not in His manifested glory when He appeared to them. The presence of Christ can go unnoticed, but when He shows up in His manifested glory, He will not go unnoticed. In verses twenty-five and twenty-six of Luke 24, Jesus speaks, "How foolish you are, and how slow of heart to believe all that the prophets have spoken! Did not the Christ have to suffer these things and then enter his glory?" These two men still did not recognize Jesus after He said these words. They finally recognized Him at the table when He gave thanks, broke the bread, and began to give it to them. Suddenly their eyes opened, and they recognized Him. Then He disappeared from their sight. Christ entered His full glory when? It states in the Word that after He suffered and died, Jesus entered His glory. Do not forget there are different levels and facets to the glory.

When Jesus called forth Lazarus from the dead, "Jesus said, 'Did I not tell you that if you believed, you would see the glory of God?' So they took away the stone. Then Jesus looked up and said, 'Father, I thank you that you have heard me. I knew that you always hear me, but I said this for the benefit of the people standing here, that they may believe that you sent me'" (John 11:40–42). After He said this, Jesus called in a loud voice, "Lazarus, come out!" This was all for the glory of God, so men might believe. This did not mean that they saw God's face or that He passed them by as He did with Moses. This was His glory revealed by the raising of Lazarus from the dead. His presence and power were being revealed to the people. The purpose for the glory shown here was for the people to see God's power being used by Jesus and then believe in Him.

Moses had an encounter with God. John the Revelator had an encounter with God. Saul, who later became Paul, had a Damascus Road encounter. These were all different living examples of God's glory demonstrated. God reveals Himself in different ways to individuals, through an ignited passion, a holy pursuit, a following hard after Him. He will take you to new levels of His manifested presence and glory.

In John 17:1–5, Jesus looked toward heaven and prayed, "Father, the time has come. Glorify your Son, that your Son may glorify you. For you granted him authority over all the people that he might give eternal life to all those you have given him. Now this is eternal life: That they may know you, the only true God, and Jesus Christ, whom you have sent. I have brought you glory on earth by completing the work you gave me to do. And now, Father, glorify me in your presence with the glory I had before the world began." *This is the glory Jesus shared with the Father before the world was created— different levels and facets of glory*. The Son waited to share the glory with the Father in heaven once again. Are you waiting to see Him in all His glory?

Let's examine the glory of God that is to be poured out upon the face of this earth. The Old Testament passage here corresponds with the New Testament. They mirror one another. Many times the old foretells the future. We read in Exodus 19:4–5, 10–12, 16–19:

How I carried you on eagles wings and brought you to myself. Now if you obey me fully and keep my covenant, then out of all the nations you will be my treasured possession.... And the Lord said Moses, "Go to the people and consecrate them today and tomorrow. Have them wash their clothes and be ready by the third day, because on that day the Lord will come down on Mount Sinai in the sight of all the people. Put limits for the people around the mountain and tell them, 'Be careful that you do not go up the mountain or touch the foot of it. Whoever touches the mountain shall surely be put to death.'... On the morning of the third day there was thunder and lighting, with a thick cloud over the mountain, and a very loud trumpet blast. Everyone in the camp trembled. Then Moses led the people out of the camp to meet with God, and they stood at the foot of the mountain. Mount Sinai was covered with smoke, because the Lord descended on it in fire. The smoke billowed up from it like smoke from a furnace, the whole mountain trembled violently, and the sound of the trumpet grew louder and louder. Then Moses spoke and the voice of God answered him.

God beckons us to Him by His Holy Spirit. When we choose to obey Him and His commands, we then become His treasured possession. God calls for a heart that is willing to obey Him fully, regardless of circumstances or events. God told the Israelites to consecrate (*set apart for sacred use*) themselves today and tomorrow. Have them wash the dirt off. Remember, a day is a thousand years to the Lord. Two days would be 2,000 years. (See Psalm 90:4.) God told them to wash their clothes or garments. This was used as an illustration to explain to them to get ready and purify themselves. For on the third day the Lord was coming. God is still calling the bride to remove all spots, wrinkles, and blemishes from her garment. Another way to say it is, "wash yourself; get rid of all filth and sin in your life." The church needs to be ready, for the third day is coming upon us quickly. Revelation 19:7–9 says the wedding of the Lamb Christ Jesus will come, and His bride will have made herself ready for Him dressed in fine, bright, white linen, which she shall wear standing for the righteous acts. The angel declares, "Blessed are those who are invited to the wedding supper of the Lamb!" Make sure you have your invitation.

When the glory of the Lord covers this earth, there will be trembling like never before as God shows Himself in His glory. Will you be ready? First Corinthians 10:1–4 says, "For I do not want you to be ignorant of the fact, brothers, that our forefathers were all under the cloud and passed through the sea. They were all baptized into Moses and in the sea. They all are and drank the same spiritual drink; for they drank from the spiritual rock that accompanied them, and that rock was Christ.

God, however, was not pleased with most of them and their bodies were scattered across the desert. This occurred as an example for us to keep us from setting our hearts on evil. We are warned not to be idolaters. In one day, twenty-three thousand died from committing sexual immorality. Then we are warned not to test the Lord our God as they did and were killed. We are also warned about grumbling as they did when the destroying angel killed them. These were given as warnings to us. Warning against pride is also mentioned. So let's beware of God's warnings and be careful that we do not fall. God will not let you be tempted beyond what you can bear, for He is faithful to His Word. Daily, we are to check our heart and see if it is pure. Abide with God daily in communication, for He will enable you to withstand temptation. Watch the words that come forth from your mouth, and guard your heart. These are examples from Israel's history of what sinful living and immoral conduct can cost an individual. God never changes, and His power does not diminish. We are the ones who are called to change ourselves. Satan goes about seeking whom he may catch off guard so he can destroy you. Do not fall into his traps. In the days that are approaching, darkness grows, but so does the light of God. The place to dwell is in the light of God. His light will grow brighter and brighter, until at last His manifested glory shall cover the earth as the waters cover the sea. We are living in the times when His glory shall be revealed.

May this be your prayer:

> *O God, hear the cry of my spirit to know Your manifested glory and dwell in that secret place with the Most High abiding under the shadow of God Almighty. Lord, abide with me all the days of my life, and teach me to be like You. I praise You for revealing new facets of Your divine nature to me each and every day. Lord, I praise You, for You keep me, and You are faithful. Thank You, Lord, for hearing the prayer of my heart. Thank You for shedding Your holy love and fear abroad in my heart along with Your divine revelation and knowledge. Father, I love You and praise You with all my heart. May Your manifested glory cover the earth as the waters cover the sea. I ask in Jesus' most precious name. Amen!*

Chapter 14

EARS TO HEAR

G OD WILL SEND messengers to prepare the way for His coming, and they will call the church to purification and sanctification. The cleansing within the church must take place before Christ's returning. Let's not forget that nothing is ever hidden from the Lord. If we could come to the revelation knowledge of His awesomeness in knowing all things, then we would trust Him fully. For we would count it joy to lay down our lives for Him. The Lord asks, "Who will surrender all to me, praying with me for unity among my body of believers? Who has ears to hear and do what I command my people?" (See John 17:23.) "If anyone considers himself religious and yet does not keep a tight rein on his tongue, he deceives himself and his religion is worthless.... Do not merely listen to the word, and so deceive yourselves. Do what it says" (James 1:26, 1:22).

Jesus states in Luke 12:2–5, "There is nothing concealed

that will not be disclosed, or hidden that will not be made known. What you have said in the dark will be heard in the daylight, and what you have whispered in the ear in the inner rooms will be proclaimed from the roofs. I tell you, my friends, do not be afraid of those who kill the body and after that can do no more. But I will show whom you should fear: fear him who, after the killing of the body, has power to throw you into hell. Yes, I tell you, fear him." Listen to this one more time, "Yes, I tell you, fear him." It does not matter what you have said or done, for nothing is hidden from God. Even those unspoken secret things you thought, He knows them all. God hears all things, knows all things, and says, "Return to me your God." He that has ears hears what God is saying. The hearing ear will hear and apply the Word of the Lord to his or her life. To hear but not apply the Word of God will cause destruction to your life.

Hear what God is saying in Malachi 3:1–3. "'See, I will send my messenger, who will prepare the way before me. Then suddenly the Lord you are seeking will come to his temple; the messenger of the covenant, whom you desire, will come,' says the LORD Almighty. But who can endure the day of his coming? Who can stand when he appears? For he will be like a refiner's fire or a launderer's soap. He will sit as a refiner and purifier of silver. He will purify the Levites and refine them like gold and silver.'" The messenger is sent to proclaim the truth. If we seek to hear the truth, we shall apply the launderer's soup to the garment of our life. Simply put, those who seek and desire shall hear and apply the washing of God's Word to their lives. Now the cleansing time has arrived, and He has commanded His bride to make ready for His return. For who that is unclean can stand before Him? His people who seek Him will be ready when He returns. His bride will be without spot, wrinkle, or blemish—completely clean.

Malachi 3:6–9 states, "'I the LORD do not change. So you, O descendants of Jacob, are not destroyed. Ever since the time of your forefathers you have turned away from my decrees and have not kept them. Return to me, and I will return to you,' says the LORD Almighty. 'But you ask, "How are we to return?" Will a man rob God? Yet you rob me. But you ask, "How do we rob you?" In tithes and offerings. You are under a curse—the whole nation of you—because you are robbing me.'" Malachi 3:3–4 states, "Then the LORD will have men who will bring offerings of righteousness, and the offerings of Judah and Jerusalem will be acceptable to the LORD, as in days gone by, as in former years." Robbing God brings curses for individuals and for the nation. God knows all things, and He changes not! He knows this scripture has not been taught correctly in some churches. Have we been turning away from bringing offerings of righteousness? Have we lived our life on the altar of sacrifice, bringing God acceptable offerings of righteousness? Can we say we brought not only the tithe to God, but also our entire being in offerings of righteousness? The tithe has been preached on, and many give unto God their tenth, yet they fail to receive the blessings of God poured out on them.

Malachi 2:11–13 tells us that those who break faith and takes up with other gods, uniting their lives with that god, are cut off from the Lord God. They may bring their tithe to the church and weep and wail, but God will not accept them, for they rob Him in offerings of righteousness. Do not unite with idols. Keep God as Lord and King over all. Having ears to hear, hear what God is saying now. Bring acceptable offerings of righteousness, bring the whole tithe—not only the tenth of your income, but all of you on the altar of sacrifice as an offering of righteousness. As in days gone by, return again to giving your all unto God.

God will direct your paths in all things. He will not lead His children astray. Pray for those who need to be set free from the grip of this world along with the love of its pleasures. Let's heed the Word of God. Reading further in Malachi 3:13–16,

"'You have said harsh things against me,' says the LORD. 'Yet you ask, "What have we said against you?" You have said, "It is futile to serve God. What did we gain by carrying out his requirements and going about like mourners before the LORD Almighty? But now we call the arrogant blessed. Certainly the evildoers prosper, and even those who challenge God escape.'" [*only momentarily until Judgment Day*]. Then those who feared the LORD talked with each other, and the LORD listened and heard. A scroll of remembrance was written in His presence concerning those who feared the LORD and honored His name." [These are the names of those who reverenced the Lord, listened and then applied the Word to their life.] To serve the Lord brings joy and a fullness that completes you. Do not grieve the Spirit of God by saying, "Its useless to serve God." Love Him with all your heart, and serve Him daily.

Malachi 3:18 and 4:1 says, "And you will again see the distinction between the righteous and the wicked, between those who serve God and those who do not. 'Surely the day is coming; it will burn like a furnace. All the arrogant and evildoer will be stubble, and that day that is coming will set them on fire,' says the LORD Almighty.'" The wicked will be destroyed, but those who revere God shall be made whole. God will judge all mankind. Do not be hearers only and not go applying the Word daily to your life. In Amos 5:14 it tells us, "Seek good, not evil, that you may live. Then the LORD God Almighty will be with you, just as you say he is." Seek the Lord so you may abide in Him and Him in you. Searching to know Him more is to hear His Word, then obey His Word. Read His Word daily, talk to God, and then listen and apply the word.

There is a call to return to God in Zechariah 1:2–6, "The LORD was very angry with your forefathers. Therefore tell the people this is what the LORD Almighty says: 'Return to me [*repent*],' declares the LORD Almighty, 'and I will return to you,' says the LORD Almighty. Do not be like your forefathers, to whom the earlier prophets proclaimed: This is what the

LORD Almighty says: 'Turn from your evil ways and your evil practices.' But they would not listen or pay attention to me, declares the LORD. Where are your forefathers now? And the prophets, do they live forever? But did not my words and my decrees, which I commanded my servants the prophets, overtake your forefathers? Then they repented and said, 'The LORD Almighty has done to us what our ways and practices deserve." Return to God, and He will return to you. Do not turn from Him; seek Him and run to Him. Do not break your covenant agreement with the Lord God Almighty. God tells us how to live and how not to live. Therefore we have no excuses to give Him.

God told Jeremiah:

> Tell them that this is what the LORD, the God of Israel, says: "Cursed is the man who does not obey the terms of this covenant—the terms I commanded your forefathers when I brought them out of Egypt, out of the iron-smelting furnace." I said, "Obey me and do everything I command you, and you will be my people, and I will be your God. Then I will fulfill the oath I swore to your forefathers, to give them a land flowing with milk and honey"—the land you possess today.... Proclaim all these words in the towns of Judah and in the streets of Jerusalem: *"Listen to the terms of this covenant and follow them.* From the time I brought your forefathers up from Egypt until today, I warned them again and again, saying, *'Obey me.'* But they did not listen or pay attention; instead, they followed the stubbornness of their evil hearts. So I brought on them all the curses of the covenant I had commanded them to follow but that they did not keep."
> —JEREMIAH 11:3–8, EMPHASIS ADDED

God has warned time and time again, "Obey Me only." There is a terrible price to pay for refusing to listen and obey.

The price is worth it to those who do obey. God's Word tells us blessed are the eyes that see the truth of His Word and the ears that hear and apply it. (See Matthew 13:16.)

In Revelation 3:1–6 it says, "To the angel of the church in Sardis [*a modern city of great wealth and fame*] write: These are the words of Him who holds the seven spirits of God and the seven stars. I know your deeds [*what has been done*]; you have a reputation of being alive, but you are dead. Wake up! Strengthen what remains and is about to die, for I have not found your deeds [*acts*] complete in the sight of my God. Remember, therefore, what you have received and heard; obey it, and repent [*turn from your sins*]. But if you do not wake up [*repent*], I will come like a thief, and you will not know at what time I will come to you. Yet you have a few people in Sardis who have not soiled their clothes [*lived in sin*]. They will walk with me, dressed in white [*my bride*], for they are worthy. He who overcomes will, like them, be dressed in white [*body of believers*]. I will never blot out his name from the book of life, but will acknowledge his name before my Father and his angels. He who has an ear, let him hear what the Spirit says to the churches." Sardis represents the churches that are modern and not humble, lowly, or meek, but rather seeking fame and fortune in the world and praise for themselves, not to God. As His sheep we are to know His voice, having ears to hear Him and follow Him.

Revelation 3:7–13 continues, "To the angel of the church in Philadelphia [*the gateway to the high central plateau, meaning, "brotherly love," loyal, and devoted*] write: These are the words of him who is holy and true, who holds the key of David. What he opens no one can shut, and what he shuts no one can open. I know your deeds [*acts*]. See, I have placed before you an open door that no one can shut. I know that you have little strength, yet you have kept my word and have not denied my name. I will make those who are of the synagogue of Satan, who claim to be Jews though they are not, but are liars—I will make them come and fall down at your feet and acknowledge that I have loved you. Since you have kept my command to endure patiently, I will also keep you from the hour of trial that is going to come upon the whole world to test those who live on earth. I am coming soon. Hold on to what you have, so that no one will take your crown. Him who overcomes I will make a pillar in the temple of my God. Never again will he leave it. I will write on him the name of my God and the name of the city of my God, the new Jerusalem, which is coming down out of heaven from my God; and I will also write on him my new name. He who has an ear, let him hear what the Spirit says to the churches.'" In Sardis, Philadelphia, and every one of the seven churches listed, it says, "He who has an ear, let him hear what the Spirit says to the churches." God is speaking to His people. Are we listening? As a body of believers, are we prepared to meet the Bridegroom? Are you ready to meet Christ? Is it your prayer to have ears that hear then obey His voice and follow Him?

> *Lord, we ask that we not only have ears to hear, but that we obey and follow only you every day. Lord, You are our Shepherd. We are the sheep called to listen to Your voice and know Your voice. Lord, let us not forget the words that we have heard, but rather apply them deep within our lives. We thank You, Lord, for the Holy Spirit that speaks to our hearts and lives revealing the truth of Your Word. Amen.*

Chapter 15

EXAMINE YOURSELF AS YOU RUN THE RACE

G OD CALLS US to strive for perfection, to be of one mind with our hearts fixed on Him. The call of God is that we surrender our lives to Him—so He can flow through us, using us for His good pleasure. The fragrance of Christ is where His aroma is and where the knowledge and life of Christ flow to you. The aroma is where His pleasing presence is noticed and captured in the atmosphere. We are called to be a fragrant offering, an acceptable sacrifice, pleasing to God. (See 2 Corinthians 2:14–16 and Philippians 4:18.) At the end of this chapter, you will find a self-test that you can take to Help you grow more Christlike.

The apostle Paul reminds us in Galatians 5:7–10, 16, "You were running a good race. Who cut in on you and kept you from obeying the truth? [*Think carefully; who did you submit to that took you off track?*] That kind of persuasion does not come from the One who calls you. A little yeast works through the whole batch of dough. I am confident in the Lord that you will take no other view. The one who is throwing you into confusion will pay the penalty, whoever he may be. Live by the Spirit so you will not gratify the desires of the sinful nature." Yeast is known as a leaven agent, to raise, arouse, or to puff up a matter. The leaven in this passage means to create a spiritual change in an individual, to puff up with proud flesh inflated. Beware of what a little bit of leaven can do to your spiritual race. The Spirit of God will reveal sin to you when you ask Him. Press on toward the goal that God has for your life in Him. Keep running the race. Stay focused on the Lord and obeying His voice. Do not be cut off from finishing your destination. When you become weary, tempted, and tried, and man is against you, remember Christ passed through the test so that He might be able to help you in your hour of testing. Beware of the fact people know when the water tide is flowing and also when it is receding. Be determined to obey and follow God as you run the race.

Philippians 3:12–16 speaks of pressing toward the goal "Not that I have already obtained all this, or have already been made perfect, but I press on to take hold of that for which Christ Jesus took hold of me. Brothers, I do not consider myself yet to have taken hold of it. But one thing I do: Forgetting what is behind and straining toward what is ahead, I press on toward the goal to win the prize for which God has called me heavenward in Christ Jesus. All of us who are mature should take such a view of things. And if on some point you think differently, that too God will make clear to you. Only let us live up to what we have already attained." God wants us to apply the truth of His Word we have already comprehended. It is simply living up to what has been deposited into our hearts and spirits. God calls us (*individually*) to work out our salvation by spiritual growth and development. This process is achieved by reading the Word, studying the Word, applying the Word, communicating with the Lord, and hearing the voice of God.

Philippians 2:12–16 says, "Therefore, my dear friends, as you have always obeyed—not only in my presence, but now much more in my absence—continue to work out your salvation with fear and trembling, for it is God who works in you to will and to act according to his good purpose. Do everything without complaining or arguing, so that you may become blameless and pure, children of God without fault in a crooked and depraved generation, in which you shine like stars in the universe as you hold out the word of life—in order that I may boast on the day of Christ that I did not run or labor for nothing." This is the importance of perseverance—ongoing laboring—singleness of mind with a set determined purpose to obtain your destination. There is a place of salvation tied to a holy fear and trembling with a deep love that flows from your life to Christ Jesus, as you yield yourself to God. Working out your salvation is based on your obedience to God, being wholeheartedly devoted to God. Are you bringing the fragrance of heaven to the world around you?

Ask yourself, "What is my assignment to fulfill here on earth? God created you with a definite purpose. Second Corinthians 13:5–9 tells us, "Examine yourselves to see whether you are in faith; test yourselves. Do you not realize that Christ Jesus is in you—unless, of course, you fail the test? And I trust that you will discover we have not failed the test. Now we pray to God that you will not do anything wrong. Not that people will see that we have stood the test, but that you will do what is right even though we may seem to have failed. For we cannot do anything against the truth, but only for the truth. We are glad whenever we are weak but you are strong; and our prayerj is for your perfection."

To sum this up, by God's power we live in Him and move and have our being. Take a moment to reflect where you are at spiritually and where you would like to be heading in your walk with Christ. Christ calls us to examine the lifetime commitment we have made to Him. When we are dependant upon God as our source of strength, we show forth our joy by relying upon Him in all things. First Thessalonians 4:1–2 says, "Finally, brothers, we instructed you how to live in order to please God, as in fact you are living. Now we ask you and urge you in the Lord Jesus to do this more and more. For you know what instructions we gave you by the authority of the Lord Jesus." Notice what should be our way of living every day—to live pleasing God. Allow the truth of "no longer I, but Christ liveth in me" to become a living reality. Let the Word strengthen and reveal to you your present position, thus leading you into a deeper walk with God Almighty. Here is a trustworthy saying in 2 Timothy 2:11–13, "If we died with him, we will also live with him; if we endure [*persevere the race*], we will also reign with him. If we disown him [*deny*], he will also disown us; if we are faithless, he will remain faithful, for he cannot disown himself."

If we have crucified the desires of our selfishness and have chosen to dwell with Christ, then we live in Him. When we endure and continue to work out our salvation—we will rule with Him. It goes on to say if we deny Him, He will deny us. If we chose to be faithless, not loyal or believing in Him, He will remain faithful to His Word, for He is God and will not lie or become unfaithful to Himself. Do not be satisfied with anything less than a real change in your nature. Submit to running the race God has set before you.

On the following page, you will find an application for the position of a dead man or woman walking with Christ—dying to self. Complete the application after praying this simple prayer:

> *Lord, let the stream of life flow through me. Let me be immersed in its ceaseless flow as I choose to run the great race set before me. Let the desire of my heart be to please You, for I want my whole life to be lived for Your glory. I*

praise You, God, that the river of life never runs dry and I may drink of its pure waters. Let the fire of Your consuming Spirit come upon me. God, take me to deeper levels in You. Let me run the race before me and finish the race hearing the words, "Well done, My faithful child." I glorify Your name, Lord, thanking You for the strength You give me day to day. Amen!

APPLICATION FOR POSITION (DYING TO SELF)

Today's date: _____

Name:

_____

Address:

_____

Date of spiritual birth (required before applying):

_____

Present spiritual condition:

_____

Who is first in your life today?

_____

Position applied for:

_____

Availability:

Temporary/When convenient ❏ Part-time ❏ Full-time ❏

What do you know about this position?

_____

Are you willing to die to self?

_____

Desired spiritual condition:

_____

The call from God is for believers to die to self and surrender themselves completely to Him. This is a call to brokenness, cleansing, and total obedience to the Master. Are you ready to give up your agendas for His divine purpose and will in your life?

Chapter 16

The Father's Will or Yours?

AS LONG AS you choose to stay crucified and your will is surrendered to the will of the Father, you are covered by His blood and overshadowed with His love. The definition of will is the power to choose what one wants to do or a free choice of action. The Word says, "He who does the will of God will enter the kingdom of heaven" (Matt. 7:21). Surrendering your will to the will of the Father is of great importance. We will read many scriptures on doing the will of the Father. Jesus, speaking in Matthew 7:21–23, says, "Not everyone who says to me, 'Lord, Lord,' will enter the kingdom of heaven, but only he who does the will of my Father who is in heaven. Many will say to me on that day, 'Lord, Lord, did we not prophesy in your name, and in your name drive out demons and perform many miracles?' Then I will tell them plainly, 'I never knew you. Away from me, you evildoers!'"

The greatest obstacle in doing the will of the Father is that we have not given up our self-will. Take a moment and ponder what Jesus said here. Only he who does the will of the Father will enter the kingdom of heaven.

When Jesus walked on earth, He prayed, daily to only do the Father's will. Christ, our living example, displayed death to self—daily. We need to pray as He prayed daily submitting ourselves to the Father's will, not our own. Jesus states again in Matthew 12:50, "For whoever does the will of my Father in heaven is my brother and sister and mother." The person who does the will of the Father becomes a brother or sister in Christ Jesus and will be counted among the believers in the kingdom of heaven. Until you no longer exalt self, but commit yourself to doing only the will of God and counting yourself as nothing, God is not your all in life. The perfect will of God is found in the deep waters of life; there you will find a great peace of soul that surpasses all understanding. For when you are led by the Holy Spirit in the perfect will of God, your purpose and destiny of life will be found. In John 6:38 Jesus says, "For I have come down from heaven not to do my will but to do the will of him who sent me." He knew that God had a plan and purpose in life, and He was going to fulfill it.

How many of us have this same attitude? Have we come to the place in our lives of pleasing God, no longer pleasing man? In living the life pleasing to God, Paul says, "It is God's will that you should be sanctified; [free from sin, made holy] that you should avoid sexual immorality; that each of you should learn to control his own body in a way that is holy and honorable, not in passionate lust like the heathen, who do not know God; and that in this matter no one should wrong his brother or take advantage of him. The Lord will punish men for all such sins, as we have already told you and warned you. For God did not call us to be impure, but to live a holy life. Therefore, he who rejects this instruction does not reject man but God, who gives you his Holy Spirit" (1 Thess. 4:3–8). Once again we are instructed on what the will of God is for us—to be sanctified, holy, and honorable. The Holy Spirit is sent to convict you. When you reject His correction, you reject God. If we would bind our will to the will of the Father and loose His perfect plan for our lives on earth, we would see a great move of God across this world. Set yourself to obeying God. Let your motto be, *I surrender my will completely to God in all things.* For this is what the precious blood of my Redeemer has taught me. God from the beginning joined together submission of will, obedience, and the blood of the cross, which lead us to the fullness of life in Him.

Paul went on to warn us in Ephesians 5:15–17, "Be very careful, then, how you live—not as unwise but as wise, making the most of every opportunity, because the days are evil. Therefore do not be foolish, but understand what the Lord's will is." Submitting yourself to God means to walk in His will. Now that we have discussed cleansing and purifying your heart, binding the sin in your life, and doing the will of the Father, choose to live wisely following the perfect will of God in your life and receiving His instructions daily. "God opposes the proud but gives grace to the humble. Submit yourselves, then, to God. Resist the devil, and he will flee from you. Come near to God and he will come near to you. Wash your hands, you sinners, and purify your hearts, you double-minded" (James 4:6–8). God opposes those full of pride, the ones full of self-effort, self-confidence, self-assuredness, and self-will. So turn back from all your religious self-efforts and yield your will humbly before the Lord. To be humble means to have a meek nature, not exalting oneself, one who has submitted to God's authority. The choice is ours whether or not we give up ourselves totally to God. Your free choice determines where you spend eternity.

Jesus had no problem giving up His all for us. We read im Matthew 26:38–44:

Then He [Jesus] said to them, "My soul is overwhelmed with sorrow to the point of death. Stay here and keep watch with me." Going a little farther, he fell with his face to the ground and prayed, "My Father, if it is possible, may this cup be taken from me. Yet not as I will, but as you will." Then he returned to his disciples and found them sleeping. "Could you men not keep watch with me for one hour?" he asked Peter. "Watch and pray so that you will not fall into temptation. The spirit is willing, but the body is weak." He went away a second time and prayed, "My Father, if it is not possible for this cup to be taken away unless I drink it, may your will be done." When he came back, he again found them sleeping, because their eyes were heavy. So he left them and went away once more and prayed the third time, saying the same thing.'"

Jesus was focused on only doing the will of the Father. He was a man of prayer, and still is. He prayed three times during the hours before His death, always doing the will of the Father. He also warned His disciples to be on guard or look out and to commune with God. Do this so you will not fall into the temptation of sin. Are you following the Father's will or yours? How slow are we to see that God's will and way is the much better way.

Jesus said in John 4:34, "My food is to do the will of him who sent me and to finish his work." Jesus compared doing the Father's will and finishing His assignment to nourishment for His life. Your soul will be in harmony with God when your will lines up with His will. Then you will have intimate fellowship and delight in Him to feed your soul. In John 7:16–18, Jesus said, "My teaching is not my own. It comes from him who sent me. If anyone chooses to do God's will, he will find out whether my teaching comes from God or whether I speak on my own. he who speaks on his own does so to gain honor for himself, but he who works for the honor of the one who sent him is a man of truth; there is nothing false about him." Jesus' teaching was from the Father, not His own selected words. He came to do the work of the Father by honoring Him. When we walk in the will of the Father, we will speak the words of the Father. Jesus was submitted to the Father's will 100 percent. Jesus did great works because of His total confidence and knowledge of His Father. He knew He could completely depend on the character of God who changes not. Romans 12:2 commands us, "Do not conform any longer to the pattern of this world, but be transformed by the renewing of your mind. Then you will be able to test and approve what God's will is—his good, pleasing and perfect will." This is how we line ourselves to God's will and not to the patterns or parade of the world. Literally we march to the beat of a different drum. It is lovely to walk in the will of God, for when He leads, our steps are in perfect unity. The question is, "Who is willing to consecrate themselves today to the Lord?" To transform means to change your inner nature or character. The renewing of the mind means to begin again by bringing back into use, to restore or revive the Lord's commands in your life. The transforming and renewing of the mind is where revival springs forth. The word *revive* or *renew* stems from the word *revival,* meaning a returning to life, as awakening. When we call for revival, we are saying, "We want to return to living a life obeying Your commands, to walk only according to Your will, God."

First Chronicles 28: 9 says, "And you, my son Solomon, [*insert your name here*] acknowledge the God of your father, and serve him with wholehearted devotion and with a willing mind, for the Lord searches every heart and understands every motive behind the thoughts. If you seek him, he will be found by you; but if you forsake him, he will reject you forever." The power of the will of man was meant to yield or cooperate with the Father to receive his perfect will imparted to man. So serve God with a sincere dedicated devotion. Matthew 6:9–10 tells us, "This, then, is how you should pray: 'Our Father in heaven, hallowed be your name, your kingdom come, your will be done on earth as it is in heaven.'" This portion of the Lord's Prayer speaks of God's will being completed in your life. Is your will bound to the will of the Father? When we bind our will to the Father's will, all things become clear. To the man or woman seeking to live wholly in the will of God, death to self is the requirement.

When asked what was the greatest commandment, Jesus answered, "Love the Lord your God with all your heart and with all your soul and with all your mind" (Matt. 22:37). That covers the entire being of man in total surrender to the Lord. Lay down all of you, as you commit to His will. These truths are clearly written. One thing I want to leave you with, and that is, never get out of the will of the Father.

> *Lord, my prayer daily is to die to self and walk according to Your divine will in my life. Christ our living example fasted, prayed, emptied Himself of self, being yielded to You, even to the point of dying on the cross for me. Lord, I desire to have the same surrendered will abiding in me that Christ displayed as our living example.*

Jesus says in John 12:49–50, "For I did not speak of my own accord, but the Father who sent me commanded me what to say and how to say it. I know that his command leads to eternal life. So whatever I say is just what the Father has told me to say." Christ made the keeping of God's commands the object of His life. Will you do the same? We are to take God's will and make it our own. The power of the will of man is the choice of action you choose to embrace. Giving yourself to God's will is where you find the life of completeness.

Chapter 17

UNLOCKING THE POWER: PRAYER AND FASTING

THE EVER-FLOWING FOUNTAIN of pure love, mercy, and grace is found in God. Jesus Christ became the reservoir storing the fullness of God's love, mercy, and grace, and He made a way for us. The powerful Holy Spirit is the stream of living water, flowing from the throne room of God. We as God's children are to be the channels through which this divine love of the Father, grace of Christ Jesus, and powerful operation of the Holy Spirit are to be imparted to the world around us. The more we are connected to Christ Jesus, the more the water will flow unhindered. We are to be connected to the One who lives to intercede and to be occupied with the fullness of Christ. As you give yourself up and converse with the Holy Trinity, the waters of life will flow through you to the thirsty souls in need.

129

The joy of seeing souls transformed and the church arise will occur all through prayer.

We are going to review different types of prayers mentioned in the Bible. The first set of prayers is found in John 17. This prayer is so awesome because it reveals the prayer from the Son of God to His heavenly Father. Jesus looks toward heaven as He prayed, "Father, the time has come. Glorify your Son, that your Son may glorify you. For You granted him authority over all the people that he might give eternal life to all those you have given him. Now this is eternal life: that they may know you, the only true God, and Jesus Christ, whom you have sent. I have brought you glory on earth by completing the work you gave me to do. And now, Father, glorify me in your presence with the glory I had with you before the world began'" (John 17:1–5). The opening statement reads, "The time has come. Glorify your Son, that your Son may glorify you." Jesus completed His work, giving God all the glory. God is to get all the glory, not anyone else but God, for the work He assigns for us to do in His name. No one can teach like Jesus our teacher, for He knows what prayer is. In heaven prayer is still His beloved work. The assignment of work is now ours to bring glory to the Father's name.

Jesus prays for His disciples in John 17:6–19. A portion of that prayer (vv. 13–19) says, "I am coming to you now, but I say these things while I am still in the world, so that they may have the full measure of my joy within them. I have given them your word and the world has hated them, for they are not of the world any more than I am of the world. My prayer is not that you take them out of the world but that you protect them from the evil one. They are not of the world, even as I am not of it. Sanctify them by the truth; your word is truth. As you sent me into the world, I have sent then into the world. For them I sanctify myself, that they too may be truly sanctified." The word *sanctify* means to be free from sin, to make holy. Insert "free from sin" in place of "sanctify". "Free them from sin by the reality of your word as I, their living example, lived sanctified." When we embrace the truth of His Word, we remove the sin from our lives that has kept us separated from Him. The more fully we submit ourselves to Him, the cleaner we become. The Word of God is powerful and sharper than any word of mere man. The Word is transforming and changes individuals, bringing them continually closer to God.

Jesus continues praying for all believers in John 17:20–24, "My prayer is not for them alone. I pray also for those who believe in me through their message, that all of them may be one, Father, just as you are in me and I am in you. May they also be in us so that the world may believe that you have sent me. I have given them the glory that you gave me, that they may be one as we are one: I in them and you in me. May they be brought to complete unity to let the world know that you sent me and have loved them even as you have loved me. Father, I want those you have given me to be with me where I am, and to see my glory, the glory you have given me because you loved me before the creation of the world." The Lord emphasized the importance of believers being one. Unity, as the Trinity displays, is a completeness of walking together as one. The word *glory* used here means honor, praise, adoration, ardent devotion, splendor or brilliance, to shed radiance, and to exult triumphantly. This earthly definition gives a slight insight into what the word means, but is quite limited at best.

Persevering prayer is something Jesus did continually as He walked upon earth. He is our living example. We need to understand that prayer is essential if we want to move forward with God. Jesus gave us examples on how to pray in the Bible. Prayer and fasting is taught by our Lord in Matthew 6:9–18. Jesus said, "This, then, is how you should pray: 'Our Father in heaven, hallowed [*holy*] be your name, your kingdom [*power*]come, your will [*declaration*] be done on earth as it is in heaven. Give us today our daily bread. Forgive us our debts, as we also have forgiven our debtors. And lead us not into temptation, but deliver us from the evil one.' For if you forgive men when they sin against you, your heavenly Father will also forgive you. But if you do not forgive men their sins, your Father will not forgive your sins. When you fast, do not look somber as the hypocrites do, for they disfigure their faces to show men they are fasting. I tell you the truth, they have received their reward in full. But when you fast, put oil on your head and wash your face, so that it will not be obvious to men that you are fasting, but only to your Father, who is unseen; and your Father, who sees what is done in secret, will reward you." The passage "your will be done, on earth as it is in heaven" means God's declaration of His Word made known. We read about the will of God and His commands for mankind in the last chapter of this book. When the Lord talked about fasting, He instructed us not to look gloomy or change our appearance. In other words, maintain that cheerful-looking, peaceful presence. The outward appearance of man should not change when fasting, but rather, a closer uniting to the Lord will occur from within the man. Before fasting ask, "What is really my desire in fasting? Is it to obey fully the commands of the Father following His will for me?" When fasting and believing, are we seeking to assert our own will or submit fully to His will? God will reveal those things in your life that are not in accordance to His will as you empty yourself in prayer and fasting.

In Daniel's prayer, he turned to the Lord pleading, petitioning, and fasting for Jerusalem and Israel's people for forgiveness. Daniel 9:4–19, paraphrased, tells us that Daniel prayed to God and confessed: "O Lord, great and awesome God, you keep your covenant of love with all of those who love you and obey your commands. We acknowledge that we have sinned and done wrong. That we have been wicked and rebellious. We have not obeyed your commands and laws. We have not listened to your servants the prophets, that spoke in your name to our men in authority and to all the people of our land. Lord, you are righteous; this day we are covered with our shame—throughout the land because of our unfaithfulness to you. O Lord, we your people, country, our men in authority are covered with shame because we have sinned against you. The Lord our God is merciful and forgiving, even though we have rebelled against Him. We have not obeyed God or kept the laws He gave to us. All have sinned against your law and turned away, refusing to obey you. Now the curses and sworn judgments recorded in the law of Moses handed down have been poured out upon us because we have sinned against God. God, you have fulfilled your word spoken against us by bringing upon us great disaster. Under all of heaven nothing has ever been done like what has been done to us at this time. As it is recorded in the Law of Moses, disaster has come upon us, yet we have sought not the favor of the Lord by turning from our sins and giving attention to his truth. The Lord did not hesitate to bring the disaster upon us, for God is righteous in everything he does. We chose not to obey him. O Lord our God, you brought your people out of Egypt with your mighty hand and you made for yourself a name that lasts. We have done wrong. O Lord, in keeping with all your righteous acts, turn away your righteous anger and wrath. We your people have become an object of scorn to all those around us. God, hear the prayers and petitions of your servant. O God, hear our cry, open your eyes and see the desolation. We have not made requests of you because we are righteous, but because of your great mercy. O Lord, listen and forgive! O God, do not delay, because we your people and nation bear your name."

Daniel humbled himself in prayer, petitioning the Lord on behalf of the people of Israel and Jerusalem. This prayer can be used today as we humble ourselves in prayer, petitioning God on behalf of our nation and His people. This prayer is a good example of praying and fasting for your nation, city, and the sins of people.

Joel 2:12, 15–16 says, "'Even now', declares the LORD, 'return to me with all your heart, with fasting and weeping and mourning.... Blow the trumpet in Zion, declare a holy fast, call a sacred assembly. Gather the people, consecrate the assembly.'" A fast is a time of self-denial, repenting for sins and humbling yourself before the Lord. When you fast, clarity is greater. When you empty self, you hear from heaven, and God can move more easily through you. Isaiah 58 speaks on fasting. It is humbling yourself in surrender to hear the voice of God as He reveals His secrets to you. This passage lists the rewards of the fast. Below is a list of some of those benefits.

1. Loose the chains of injustice.

2. Set free from yokes of oppression.

3. Sharing of your provisions with the poor and needy.

4. Your light will break forth like the dawn.

5. Healings will appear quickly.

6. Your righteousness (goodness of God) will go out before you.

7. The glory of the Lord will be your rear guard.

8. You will call and the Lord will answer.

9. Your light will rise in darkness.

10. Your night will become like the noonday.

11. The Lord will guide you always.

12. In times of leanness He will satisfy your needs.

13. The Lord will strengthen your frame or body.

14. The Lord will water you and make you fruitful.

15. You will rebuild the walls of prayer and raise up the age-old foundations.

16. You will be called repairer of broken walls, restorer of dwellings.

17. You will delight in the Sabbath and call the Lord's holy day honorable.

18. You will find joy in the Lord.

19. You will ride on the heights of the land (having authority).

20. You will feast on the inheritance of your father Jacob.

This passage ends with, "The mouth of the Lord has spoken."

Psalm 66:18 warns us, "If I had cherished sin in my heart, the Lord would not have listened." The Lord will not listen to those who hold sin in their lives, so repent quickly. First Samuel 12:23 says, "As for me, far be it from me that I should sin against the LORD by failing to pray." Failing to pray is counted a sin. God hears the prayer of a clean individual who does not hold onto sin. If you feel like your prayers are not being heard, check your heart for sin. Psalm 34:15–17 says, "The eyes of the LORD are on the righteous and his ears are attentive to their cry; the face of the LORD is against those who do evil, to cut off the memory of them from the earth. The righteous cry out, and the LORD hears them; he delivers them from all their troubles." The LORD sees and hears the righteous and delivers them. The righteous are those who honor and revere the Lord, living their lives according to God's divine will. In Psalm 145:18–19, it tells us, "The LORD is near to all who call on Him, to all who call on him in truth. He fulfills the desires of those who fear him; he hears their cry and saves them." Luke 18:14 states, "For everyone who exalts himself will be humbled, and he who humbles himself will be exalted." Call out to God in reverence and awe with meekness, as you make your requests known.

As we read in the Gospels [at the Garden of Gethsemane or Mount of Olives], Jesus usually went out to pray. He asked the disciples to stay and keep watch with Him in prayer. Jesus prayed the same prayer three times, "Father, if you are willing, take this cup from me; yet not my will, but yours be done." Jesus returned to the disciples, but they were asleep, He asked them, "Could you not keep watch for one hour?" Jesus requested them to watch and pray so that they would not fall into temptation. The spirit is willing, but the body is weak. Since Jesus usually prayed to the Father at this place, Judas knew He would be at the Garden of Gethsemane. Jesus also knew the importance of prayer and surrender when He prayed that God's will be done. Jesus also was trying to teach an important lesson here to the disciples on watching and praying. He had instructed the disciples more than once to watch, stay alert and pray, as recorded in Matthew 26:36–45; Mark 14:32–42; and Luke 22:39–45. The hindrance to praying is the flesh, the selfish spirit of man that is not surrendered to God. We have covered the steps of cleansing ourselves, submitting to the will of the Father, so the fragrance of the Holy Spirit touches us and marks us. Now we are clothing ourselves in the power of corporate prayer, fasting and seeing the mighty works of the Lord completed within us and in this world.

As we read Ruth 3:1–11, let's examine it from a different perspective that will shed a different light on this passage.

One day Naomi [*see Naomi as resembling the voice of the Holy Spirit*] her mother-in-law said to her,

> "My daughter, should I not try to find a home for you, where you will be well provided for? [*If you abide in Christ and He abides in you, your home is known, and*

He provides for you.] Is not Boaz [*see Boaz as Christ*], with whose servant girls you have been a kinsman of ours? Tonight he will be winnowing [*a process of removing chaff from the grain*] barley on the threshing [*beat to separate the grain*] floor. Wash and perfume yourself, and put on your best clothes [*cleanse, purify, anoint yourself in prayer, making sure your garment is pure.*] Then go down to the threshing floor, but don't let him know you are there until he has finished eating and drinking. When he lies down, note the place where he is lying. [*Ruth's assignment was to stay alert and watch, where Boaz would lay for the night.*] [*Boaz, as a land owner, was to spend the night in watch to protect His grain from theft.*] Then go and uncover his feet and lie down. He will tell you what to do."

"I will do whatever you say," Ruth answered. So she went down to the threshing floor and did everything her mother-in-law told her to do [*this represented her request to be married to Boaz-Christ*].

When Boaz had finished eating and drinking and was in good spirits, he went over to lie down at the far end of the grain pile. Ruth approached quietly, uncovered his feet and lay down. [*She watched and stayed alert, to keep an eye on where he would rest for the night.*] In the middle of the night something startled the man, and he turned and discovered a woman lying at his feet.

"Who are you?" he asked.

"I am your servant Ruth," she said. "Spread the corner of your garment over me, since you are a kinsman-redeemer." [*Spread your wings across me, Lord my Redeemer, protect me under your wings of protection.*]

"The Lord bless you, my daughter," he replied. "This kindness is greater than that which you showed earlier: You have not run after the younger men, whether rich or poor [*things of the world and the desires of the world*]. And now, my daughter, don't be afraid. I will do for you all you ask. [*She humbled herself, so she was about to be blessed.*]

All my fellow townsmen know that you are a woman of
noble character [*outstanding godly character.*]"

This passage covers the essence of staying alert, watching,
abiding with the Lord, and humbling ourselves before Him.
It also represents us coming before Him, bowing down at the
feet of the Master in a relationship of constant fellowshiping, a
holy marriage to Him.

As we examine the next passage, refer back to the benefits
obtained while fasting. You will see a correlation of how
the benefits can sustain you when battling with the enemy.
Matthew 4:1–2 tells us, "Then Jesus was led by the Spirit into
the desert to be tempted by the devil. After fasting forty days
and forty nights, he was hungry." Luke 4:1–2 records, "Jesus,
full of the Holy Spirit, returned from the Jordan and was led by
the Spirit in the desert, where for forty days he was tempted by
the devil." If you feel like you are having a desert experience, it
may be time to fast and pray. The children of Israel had forty
years of testing in the desert to see what was in their heart,
whether they would obey God's commands or reject them.
Jesus, on the other hand, led by the Spirit and full of the Spirit,
fasted forty days and forty nights, praying and listening to the
voice of God. So when He entered the desert to be tempted, He
overcame all the temptations the devil threw at Him. Jesus was
and is our living example of how to overcome the enemy and
live a life that is full in Him.

Jesus is the Bridegroom and, He is coming back for the bride.
He also instructs the bride to be pure, without spot, wrinkle, or
blemish upon her garment. "But the time will come when the
Bridegroom will be taken from them; in those days they will
fast" (Luke 5:35). Jesus was explaining fasting to the bride; the
bridegroom has not come to capture the bride away with Him
yet. So while she waits for her Bridegroom, the bride should be
cleansing her garment, fasting, praying, praising, worshiping
and glorifying God. These are just a few of the things the bride,

body of Christ, should be actively doing in unity together as one. We are to be unified as one with Christ Jesus our Lord, not separated by religious denominations. There is coming a time soon when the body will come together in unity, a holy unity led by the Spirit of God Almighty.

John 2:17 says, "Zeal for your house will consume me." Zeal means intense enthusiasm or passion for a cause. If we have a passion with intense enthusiasm for God's house, His holy temple, it will consume us or overtake us. For our God is a consuming fire. Colossians 4:2 tells us, "Devote [*set apart, dedicate*] yourselves to prayer, being watchful and thankful." Sometimes as believers, we just do not know what to say as we pray for certain situations or people. This is when we need to rely on the Spirit to intercede for us. As Romans 8:26–27 states, "We do not know what we ought to pray for, but the Spirit himself intercedes for us with groans that words cannot express. And he who searches our hearts knows the mind of the Spirit, because the Spirit intercedes for the saints in accordance with God's will." Let's read that again; "The Spirit intercedes for the saints in accordance with God's will." The Spirit prays the will of God. This is how we are to pray.

Paraphrasing verse 34 of Romans chapter 8, Christ is at the right hand of God interceding for us. That is where He has been since He ascended to heaven. His actions show the importance of prayer overlooked by many. Not only does Jesus still pray, but He also was a man who wept and prayed here on earth. Jesus was moved to great sorrow near to the point of death in the garden praying. "In anguish, he prayed more earnestly, and his sweat was like drops of blood falling to the ground" (Luke 22:44). Who was He praying for? For you and me, and He is praying for you and me today. He still calls, "Come and watch and pray with Me that you may not fall into temptation." He asks, "Why are you sleeping? Get up and pray!" Pray without ceasing; pray daily and seek God, lest you fall into sinning. When you become unfaithful in your prayer life, then Satan is not concerned about suffering much loss to His kingdom. Satan's plan is to distract you from your prayer time with God. Do not allow your channel to become stopped up and cause the waters to cease from flowing freely.

Chapter 18

GOD INHABITS YOUR PRAISES

GOD INHABITS (*LIVES in or dwells in*) the praises of His people. In this chapter we will be examining several passages on praise and worship and the essence of praising, worshiping, and abiding in the presence of God. Remember that God dwells in the praises of His people. Psalm 46:4 describes it this way, "There is a river whose streams make glad the city of God, the holy place where the Most High dwells." The river here serves as a metaphor for the continual outpouring and refreshing of praise and worship offered up to the city of God. When we offer up our praise to God, it enters into the city of God or the holy place where the Most High dwells (*lives in*). "God has ascended amid shouts of joy [*God will come when we lift our voices of praise and worship up to Him*], the LORD amid the sounding of trumpets. Sing praises to God, sing praises; sing praises to our King, sing praises. [*This was repeated in this scrip-*

ture to emphasize the importance of praise.] For God is the King of all the earth; sing to him a psalm of praise. God reigns over the nations; God is seated on his holy throne" (Ps. 47:5–8).

If you have an intense longing for God—a thirst that just cannot be quenched and a hunger for more of Him—get into praising and worshiping God. Abide in the place of utter joy, praising God your Creator. For in the middle of deep heartfelt praise, God will arise. Psalm 63:1–5 says, "O God, you are my God, earnestly I seek [*strive for, searching*] you; my soul thirsts for you, my body longs for you, in a dry and weary land where there is no water. I have seen you in the sanctuary and beheld your power and your glory. Because your love is better than life, my lips will glorify you. I will praise you as long as I live, and in your name I will lift up my hands. My soul will be satisfied [*fulfilled*] as with the richest of foods [*nourishment*]; with singing lips my mouth will praise you." This kind of praise starts out searching and striving after God when the soul is in need and longs for nourishment. With the eyes of your soul, you see the Lord Most High, beholding His power, glory, and abundant love, which are better than life. The soul sings out as your lips start glorifying the King Most High. The soul feasts upon the richest of foods because it proclaims praises to the Lord Most High. The prescription is to be administered by daily lifting up your voices to the Most High God. Let the songs of praises continually be in your mouth day and night.

John 4:23–24 tells us, "Yet a time is coming and has now come when the true worshipers will worship the Father in spirit and truth, for they are the kind of worshipers the Father seeks. God is spirit, and his worshipers must worship in spirit and in truth." Worship means an expression of reverence toward a divine or supernatural power, which we know is God. Worship involves showing adoration of your deep love toward Him, in singing praises, praying, living a life devoted to the King Most High. Let your spirit within you sing out to His Spirit. Psalm 95:6, 1–2, commands, "Come, let us bow down in worship, let us kneel before the LORD our Maker. Come, let us sing for joy to the LORD; let us shout aloud to the Rock of our salvation. Let us come before him with thanksgiving and extol [*praise highly*] him with music and song." Bowing down before God in humble admiration and worshiping God our Creator and King bring joy to His heart and ours. His love is like a song that penetrates your very being, mind, body, soul, and spirit. Your response to the awesomeness of His surpassing love causes your lips to sing forth praises to His holy name. Psalm 29:2 tells us, "Ascribe [attribute] to the LORD the glory due his name; worship the LORD in the splendor of his holiness." Give to the LORD the glory due to Him by singing praises to Him. Praise His great and awesome Name for HE IS HOLY! Psalm 9:1–2 says, "I will praise you, O LORD, with all my heart [*everything that is within you praises Him*]; I will tell of all your wonders. I will be glad and rejoice in you; I will sing praise to your name, O Most High."

Express from all that is within you how great and wonderful God is. When we worship Him, we are proclaiming loudly how deeply we love and adore Him. Psalm 145:21, 1–3 says, "My mouth will speak in praise of the LORD. Let every creature praise his holy name for ever and ever....I will exalt you, my God the King; I will praise your name for ever and ever. Every day I will praise you and extol your name for ever and ever. Great is the LORD and most worthy of praise; his greatness no one can fathom [*understand the depth of*]." In times of praise and worship to God, ask yourself, *"Am I wholly devoted to Him?"* Psalm 134:1–2 and 135:1–3 say, "Praise the LORD, all you servants of the LORD who minister by night in the house of the LORD. Lift up your hands in the sanctuary and praise the Lord. [*All the servants of the LORD are called to praise with uplifted hands.*] Praise the LORD. Praise the name of the LORD; praise him, you servants of the LORD, you who minister in the house of the LORD, in the courts of the house of God. Praise the LORD, for the LORD is good; sing praise to his name, for that is pleasant."

The Lord delights in our praise. It brings joy to Him when we honor Him in worship. The Lord dwells in praise; even the angels' work is to praise Him day and night. In the sweet sound of worshiping the Lord, He in turn, fills us with more of His love. He pours out into us as we pour ourselves out to Him. Psalm 149:1–4 instructs us to, "Praise the LORD. Sing to the LORD a new song, his praise in the assembly of the saints. Let Israel rejoice in their Maker; let the people of Zion be glad in their King. Let them praise his name with dancing and make music to him with tambourine and harp. For the LORD takes delight in his people; he crowns the humble with salvation." Psalm 150:1–6 states, "Praise the LORD. Praise God in his sanctuary; praise him in his mighty heavens. Praise him for his acts of power; praise him for his surpassing greatness. Praise him with the sounding of the trumpet, praise him with the harp and lyre, praise him with tambourine and dancing, praise him with strings and flute, praise him with the clash of cymbals, praise him with resounding cymbals. Let everything that has breath [*if you are alive you qualify*] praise the LORD. Praise the LORD."

A passionate affection springs forth from your spirit man as you abide in God's presence worshiping Him. In the atmosphere of praise as you honor Him, worship the King, and dance before Him in adoration, you will find the perfume of His presence. God lives in our adoration and praise of His magnificent, glorious name. Let songs of love flow out from you to Him in deep appreciation of His unending love. Matthew 26:30 and Mark 14:26 say, "When they had sung a hymn they went out to the Mount of Olives." Jesus, leading the disciples in worship, sang after partaking of the Lord's Supper. This was the conqueror singing, worshiping out of joy for the work was to be fully completed. The song of joy resounded from Him because the souls of mankind were about to be redeemed.

Jesus knew that God always triumphs, and He praised His Father in song. Christ Jesus, our living example, knowing He would be rejected and disowned, lifted His voice in a song of praise to God the night before He was crucified on the cross. In the midst of His last few hours with the disciples, He taught them to praise God in all things and to pray. To count it all joy, regardless. To praise God in song, so that His joy may abide in you. Abide with Christ, counting all things joyful, so that your joy may be full knowing God triumphs. Through Jesus our Savior, let us continually offer to God the sacrifice of praise, the fruit of our lips giving Him praise and honor. Luke 19:37–38 tells us the disciples even knew to praise Him. The entire crowd of disciples raised their voices, joyfully praising God for all the miracles they had witnessed, declaring to the Lord, "Blessed is the King who comes in the name of the Lord!" *(Acknowledging that Jesus came, sent by God.)* "Peace in heaven and glory in the highest!" (*Glorifying God, praising Him for sending Jesus.*)

John writes in Revelation 5:13, "Then I heard every creature in heaven and on earth and under the earth and on the sea, and all that is in them, singing: 'To him who sits on the throne and to the Lamb be praise and honor and glory and power, for ever and ever!'" There is coming a day when all creation shall praise His holy name, so why not start now and draw closer to Him. The life of Christ should spring forth from your inner being, where you are united as one with Him in God. The ability to remain in that secret place comes from maintaining a deep dependence and intimate fellowship with the Father. Stay united, and abide in a life of total loyalty, daily communicating to Him, grounded completely in His holy love, worshiping the King. Pour out your Love of Him in intimate worship to Him.

Hebrews 12:25–28 instructs us, "See to it that you do not refuse him who speaks. If they did not escape when they refused him who warned them on earth, how much less will we, if we turn away from him who warns us from heaven? At that time His voice shook the earth, but now he has promised, [*God is promising*] 'Once more I will shake not only the earth but also the heavens.' The words 'once more' indicate the removing of what can [*wants or allows its self*] be shaken—that is, created things—[*You are His creation*] so that what cannot be shaken may remain [*those who refuse may remain*]. Therefore, since we are receiving a kingdom that cannot be shaken, let us be thankful, and so worship [*praise and exalt*] God acceptably with reverence and awe. For our "God is a consuming fire." *God changes not—do you change?*

NOTES

Chapter 1
Absolutely Surrendered

1. Oral Roberts University Chapel, television program #76, 1974. Quest for Revival Video, "I Believe in Miracles."

Chapter 3
Godlessness or Godliness?

1. Kathryn Kuhlman, *A Glimpse Into Glory* (Gainesville, FL: Bridge-Logos Publishers, 1998), 116.

Chapter 5
Keys to God's House

1. Kuhlman, *A Glimpse Into Glory,* 116.